This is for the CLEVER KIDS
Who have a way with words,
Can write them in a class book
But out loud they are not heard.

This is for FORGOTTEN YOUTHS
Who might be “failing” school,
Except for art and music,
Which are vital *and* so cool.

This is for the DAUGHTERS
Told “Grow up” and “Act your age.”
But inside they are timeless,
Their souls on a different page.

This is for the SONS
Who are thought to lack emotion—
Yet injustice makes their insides ache;
Their hearts could drown an ocean.

This is for the FATHERS
Struggling for far too long.
No awareness that their neurotype
Has been divergent all along.

This is for the MOTHERS
Forced to pretend their whole lives.
No piece of paper to explain
This *thing* they feel inside.

This is for the TEENAGERS
Learning how to own their skin.
Their bodies, emotions, and their minds—
It's a race they'll one day win.

This is for ATYPICAL BEINGS
Who don't care if they fit.
Smart and shy and silly and strange—
There's no box in which they sit.

This is for **EXTRAORDINARY MINDS**
Who are going to change the world.
Artists, actors, activists—
Their voices *will* be heard.

This is for **EVERYONE**
Who's been called "weirdo" at school.
Maybe we're not really weird . . .
Just a different kind of normal.

This is for **ANYONE**
Who has ever felt out of place.
You don't have to be the "odd one out."
You're unique and that's just great.

For everyone who has ever felt
a different kind of normal

 Published in the United States by Crown Books for Young Readers, an imprint of Random House Children's Books, a division of Penguin Random House LLC, New York. Originally published by Puffin Books, London, in 2021.

Crown and the colophon are registered trademarks of Penguin Random House LLC.

Visit us on the Web! rhcbooks.com

Educators and librarians, for a variety of teaching tools, visit us at RHTeachersLibrarians.com

Library of Congress Cataloging-in-Publication Data is available upon request.
ISBN 978-0-593-56645-9 (hardcover)—ISBN 978-0-593-56648-0 (paperback)—
ISBN 978-0-593-56646-6 (lib. bdg.)—ISBN 978-0-593-56647-3 (ebook)

The text of this book is set in 10.1-point Alkes Light.
The illustrations in this book were created digitally.

MANUFACTURED IN SINGAPORE
10 9 8 7 6 5 4 3 2 1
First American Edition

Random House Children's Books supports the First Amendment and celebrates the right to read.

My Real-Life COMPLETELY True Story About Being UNIQUE

A Different Kind of Normal

ABIGAIL BALFE

CROWN BOOKS FOR YOUNG READERS
NEW YORK

CONTENTS

Here is a list of places we will visit in this book (because we all know autistic people love lists[1]) . . .

A Memory	5
An Introduction	7
Science, History & Facts	18
Abigail's World Map	30
School (toilets feature heavily)	34
Special Interests	50
Emotions	58
Family	66

1. JOKE! That was a classic autism stereotype. You'll find a few more of those in this book too. And you'll also find a much more interesting map of this book on page 30.

Sensory Sensitivities 74

Social Communication 97

Humor 106

Friendships 113

Big School 162

Puberty 178

College 204

My Tips for Navigating the Neurotypical World if You Are Not Neurotypical 210

My Tips for Helping an Autistic Person Feel Seen 212

My Absolute Best Things About Being Autistic 214

A Final Note 216

Really Useful Further Learning 224

Glossary 227

A MEMORY

For my **fourth birthday** my parents arranged a puppet show and invited the other children from my playgroup.

I remember watching the video of this party a few years later. While the other children sat in rows, jumping up and down, pushing to be closest to the action, I wouldn't look. I didn't understand it. And I didn't understand the other children's animated reactions to it.

I walked to the back of our living room, picking up objects and putting them down, trying my best to ignore what was going on in our home, pretending these unpredictable people and puppets were not really there, that I could carry on as normal, keep a straight face, and block out the confusing sights and sounds and smells until they simply DISAPPEARED . . .

A few months ago, I asked my mom why she had planned the puppet show party, knowing that bringing any sort of boisterous social activity into our home was extremely out of character.

"I thought that's what normal children liked," she said.

AN INTRODUCTION

(how formal)

This is a book for **everyone.**

Yes . . . **everyone.**

So that definitely means **YOU.**

No, not the person behind you on the bus. Or the child to the left of you in the playground. Or that loud neighbor you can hear shouting at their dog for the twenty-second time today.

Although, actually—yes, it **is** for them too. But right now **YOU** are the person I'm interested in talking with. And I'm very glad you are here. Thank you.

Now let me ask you this:

Have you ever felt as though you are "DIFFERENT" from other people?

Perhaps you feel like you just don't "FIT IN"?

Oh, you have? Well, *same*. See, we have something in common already.

In fact, I'd challenge you to find just one person who feels happy and confident **ALL** the time. Because (spoiler alert) that's not really how growing up works. Actually, that's not how life works. And it would probably be a bit **boring** if it was!

Hello, my name is Abigail and I'm autistic.

Even though we look like two different people because one is taller and wears glasses and is technically an **adult**[2], we are both the same person—just at slightly different stages in our life.

2. I've never really felt like an "adult" and I don't think I ever will.

I spent years feeling different without knowing quite why before autism popped up to say,

—a bit like a long-lost family member who you can't believe you haven't already met because you have so much in common.

Autism is a difference in the brain that affects how a person experiences and interacts with the world around them.

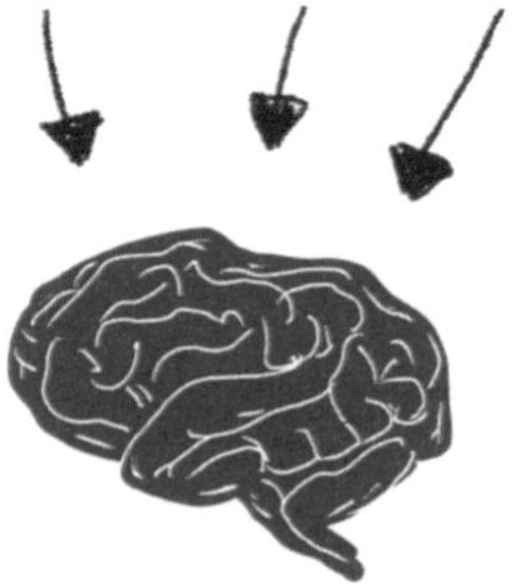

Discovering my autism as an adult-sort-of-person is what compelled me to write and illustrate this book.

This is a collection of doodles and thoughts about my experiences growing up as an autistic child. An autistic child who **didn't know** she was an autistic child.

Because if someone had told me when I was younger that it was OK to not be like everybody else, that it was not my job to try to be "normal" and to "fit in," that my way of seeing the world was just as valid and important as everybody else's, then I think I would have found growing up a lot easier.

Now, I'm not saying that if you feel out of place in the world, then you must be autistic. I'm here to tell you **MY STORY**. Which is just one story out of many.

Hopefully, through telling you my own growing-up story, I can help you see why it's actually pretty amazing to be

A DIFFERENT KIND OF NORMAL,

whatever those five words mean to you.

And if I can shed some light on autism along the way, then that would be really great too.

You see, autism can sometimes look different across the **GENDER SPECTRUM:** a colorful-sounding term that includes the many genders you may come across in daily life. Here are a few you are likely to hear most often:

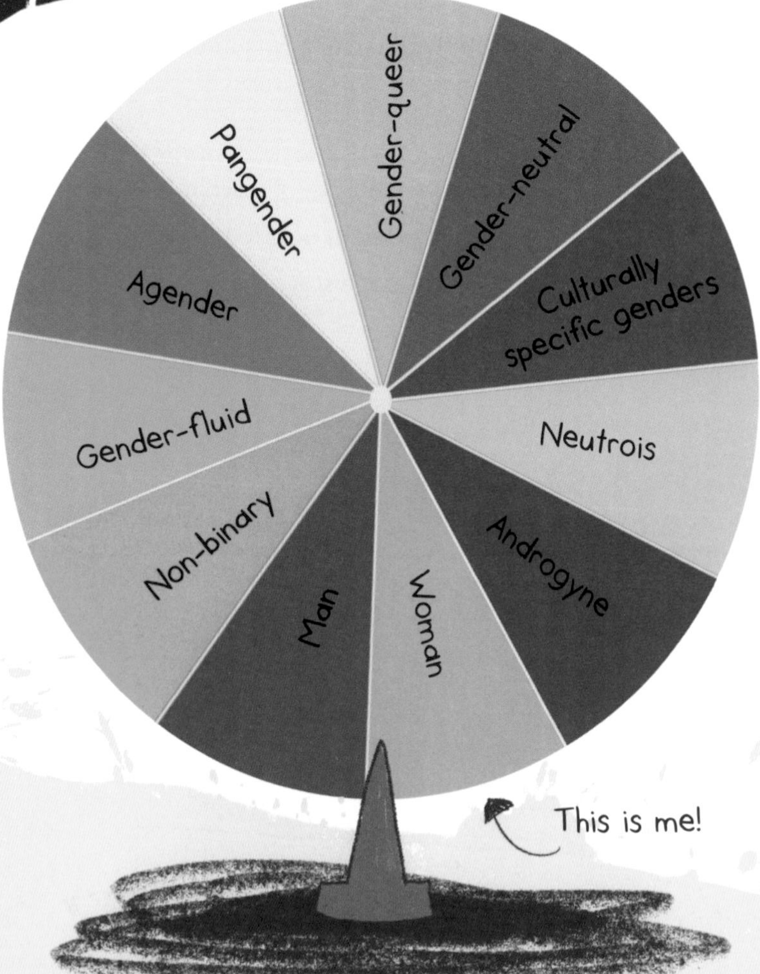

I am a cisgender woman. This means that the gender assigned to me at birth, based on my assigned sex at birth, was female and I identify as being female. (Those whose gender identity is different from the gender they were assigned at birth are transgender, and you can find out more about this on page 182.) But the system that's supposed to diagnose and support autistic people works in favor of white cisgender boys.

This means that those of us who are not white cisgender boys may not discover our autism until we have been in the world for quite a few years—if we do at all.

But, a bit like an overwhelming (yet delicious) breakfast buffet, autism is open to

EVERYONE.

However, autism is often **invisible** to the untrained (or even the trained) eye, something that is not very helpful when you are one of those autistic people attempting to make sense of the confusing world around you. (And when you just want a simple, non-challenging breakfast to see you through the day.)

SIDE NOTE: Who in their right mind (whatever that means—I'm pretty sure there isn't a "right" or "wrong" mind, just different minds, but anyway that's beside the point) made the decision to put **CUCUMBER** in a sandwich?! It's basically like eating a squashed slug inside a wet piece of cloth. **Disgusting.**

And, yes, now I'm thinking about which animals represent which food combinations best. Because, you see, my brain likes to wander off to interesting places. Most probably because I am **neurodivergent** . . .

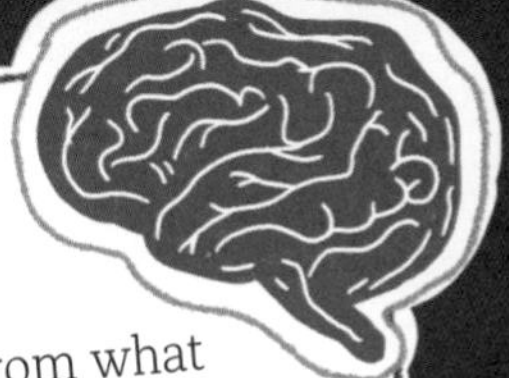

NEURODIVERGENT

Differing in brain function from what is considered typical or "normal." Examples of neurodivergence include: autism, dyspraxia, dyslexia, attention deficit hyperactivity disorder (ADHD), dyscalculia, and Tourette's syndrome. Anyone who is not neurodivergent is neurotypical.

NEUROTYPICAL

Being neurotypical is the opposite of being neurodivergent. A person who is neurotypical has a more **"typical"** way of thinking. Their brain experiences the world, and reacts to it, in a way that is largely understood by society.

NEURODIVERSITY

A word that covers the **full spectrum** of brain types and celebrates the importance of each one! This includes both neurodivergent **and** neurotypical people.

And another very important word I'll be using throughout this book:

ALLISTIC

Someone who is **NOT** autistic.

That reminds me . . . You'll be pleased to know that these helpful fact boxes are scattered throughout the book, and if you turn to the back you will find a handy glossary of important words. This is because for **some reason** when adult people write about autism they like to use complicated collections of letters and serious-sounding sentences.

I'd rather not do that, really, but I guess I can't rewrite the dictionary **as well** as writing this book, can I?!

So, yes—I hope this book helps young people and not-so-young people who are on journeys of self-discovery. Those of you who are in search of answers, comfort, or maybe just some light entertainment. Whether you are autistic or allistic, neurodivergent or neurotypical—or if you have no idea which category you fall into right now . . .

Before I tell you more about ME, I'd like us to look at autism in a bit more detail together, because my autism discovery was such a big part of me learning about myself and finding my different kind of normal . . .

Science, History & Facts

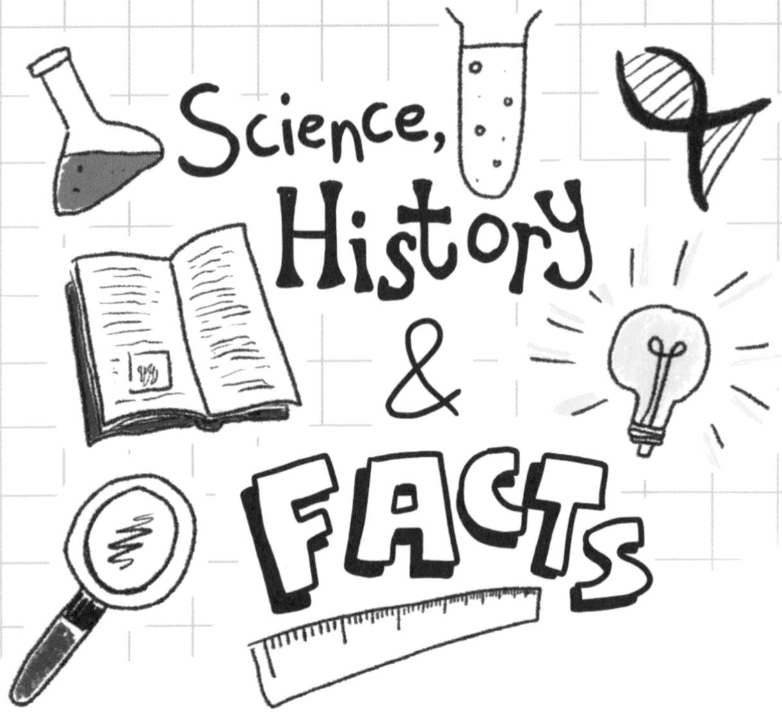

I am not a scientist, a historian, or an expert in neurological conditions. ("Neurological" means relating to the nervous system—including the brain.)

When I was at school, the teachers encouraged me to take double science because my grades were good, but I said no thanks and took art and drama instead.

I am an autistic female with a special interest in autism.

I don't want to get too heavy with facts, figures, and history because this isn't supposed to be an information book as such. However, it can be really useful to take a peek at the facts and science behind our real-life stories sometimes.

Plus, autistic people can often be quite into facts and figures and history[3], so there will be a few along the way. But mostly this is me, writing my True-Life Actual Childhood Diary, but as a "GROWN-UP" person who didn't actually have a childhood diary. Apart from the "autobiography" I started writing when I was fourteen because I thought I was going to be a famous TV star one day and I figured it would be good to get a head start.

Luckily for me, though, autistic people tend to have very good LONG-TERM MEMORIES . . .

3. Well, I'm a definite fan of these and I know lots of other autistic people who are too.

WHAT IS AUTISM?

If you search **"autism"** on the internet, one of the first results you're likely to find is the Wikipedia page and this description:

> **Autism is a developmental disorder characterized by difficulties with social interaction and communication, and by restricted and repetitive behavior. Parents often notice signs during the first three years of their child's life . . . It is diagnosed four to five times more often in males than females.**

If your eyes haven't glazed over from that definition, then congratulations—you're officially moving through this book faster than I did when I read it back just now!

So, for starters, I don't see autism as a "disorder" and neither do many autistic people and their families. Many of us see it as a developmental **difference**.

Our brains work differently from allistic brains.

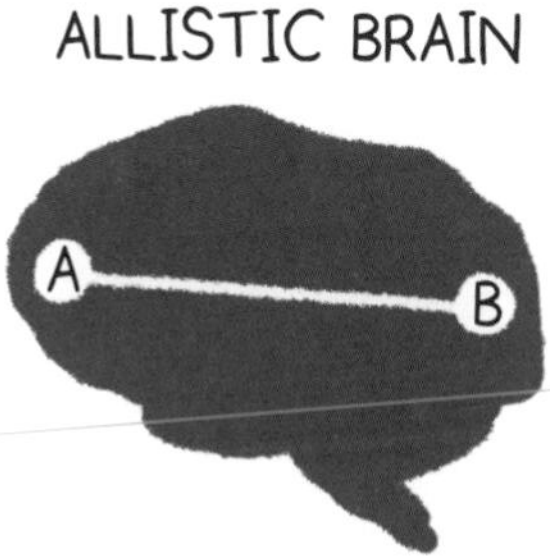

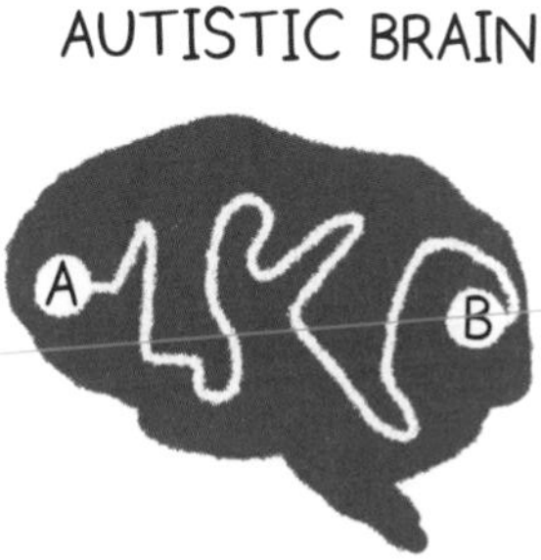

There's nothing wrong with that. Actually, there are loads of benefits to us not seeing the world in the same way as many of the people around us. Plus, who decided that the allistic brain was the ideal brain anyway?! Just because there are a few more people who AREN'T autistic in the world than those who ARE, that doesn't mean it's the right way to be, does it?

Also, my parents did not notice signs of my autism during the first three years of my life. In fact, it was me who approached my mom to say I thought I was autistic—when I was thirty-one.

This is not a unique story. It is becoming more and more common as people become more aware of the different experiences of autism.

Also, the idea that autism occurs more often in males than females is outdated and incorrect. As we know, autism can look different across the gender spectrum. Plus, people who aren't male can be a lot better at **masking**. (We'll get on to masking in a bit. Masking deserves a chapter of its very own, really . . . or at least a nice comfy seat in a quiet room on another page while we explore a few other things first.)

OK, so we all know that Wikipedia is not the most **reliable** source for health information. You don't have to be **Einstein** to work that out. (Did you know that Einstein was most probably autistic? Another reason being autistic can be **SUPER COOL**: you get to join a club with some pretty epic humans.)

But, let's face it, most people in search of a quick answer look to the first page of the internet search results. And the answers immediately available are shaping how autism is understood by the world.

It's time we CHANGED the search results.

And it's time we started asking DIFFERENT QUESTIONS.

I'LL BEGIN . . .

WHO CAN AUTISM AFFECT?

Simple answer:

ANYONE!

As you've probably guessed by now,

there is no

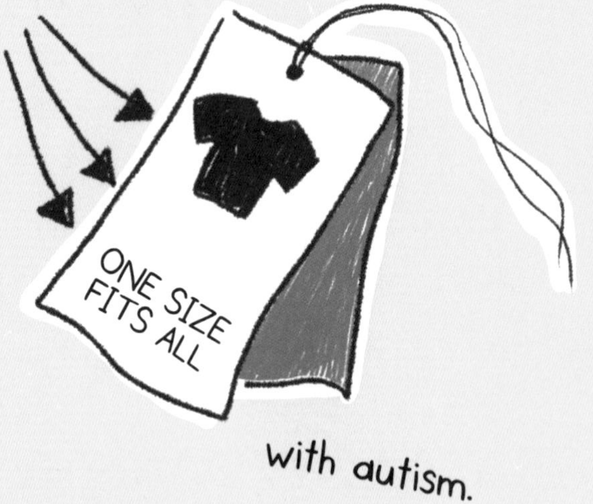

with autism.

Autism is open to all races, religions, genders, sexualities, social backgrounds, eye colors, star signs, and shoe sizes.

Um, probably not.

OR, at least, no one has done any research on that JUST yet . . .

WHAT DOES AUTISM

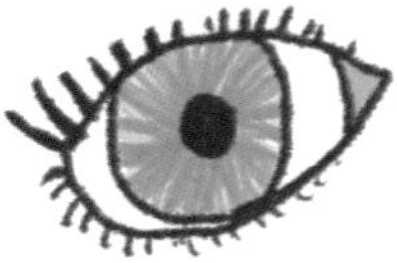

LOOK LIKE?

Well, that's a very good question. I'm glad you asked. Here are some autistic traits you might be aware of:

- ✓ Social difficulties
- ✓ Special interests
- ✓ Repetitive behavior, movement, or speech
- ✓ Difficulties with eye contact
- ✓ Dislike of change
- ✓ Reliance on strict rules and routine

But did you know that these traits can appear more obvious in the so-called **male** experience of autism?

Luckily I did **some**[4] research on this, which helped me discover I was autistic.

However, the supposed facts and figures could only get me so far. It was the video diaries, the blogs, and the photo updates from the autistic community on Instagram, Twitter, and YouTube that really helped me understand that I actually, probably (definitely) might be part of this fascinating and brilliant brain club.

4. LOTS of research.

My research on the "female" experience of autism led me to make this diagram . . .

and to post it on Instagram.

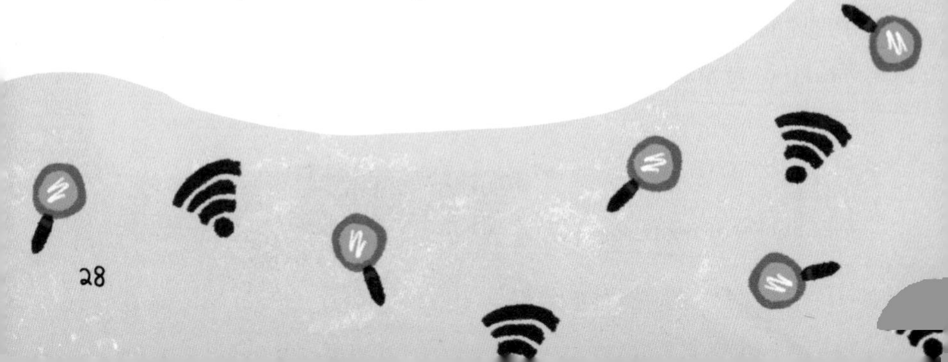

It became obvious that I was not the only one who could relate to these lesser-known autistic traits. And I soon learned that these traits are **NOT** limited to just girls.

I realized pretty soon that I needed to do a few more drawings and diagrams and maybe even a few words too.

And here we are.

THIS BOOK

is those drawings and diagrams and words.

I THINK REAL STORIES ARE IMPORTANT.

So is science and history and research. But real stories draw us in and confirm the things we've been told, or challenge our views and make us think in a different way.

Every autistic person is different. If you know one autistic person, then you know one autistic person. **BUT** learning about autism through the eyes of an autistic person can be extremely helpful, illuminating . . . and in some cases vital.

ABIGAIL'S WORLD MAP
SENSORY SENSITIVITIES
Page 74
MASKING
Page 170
SCHOOL
Page 34
Page 66
FAMILY
SCHOOL SUBJECTS
Page 58
EMOTIONS

CATS
Page 97
SOCIAL COMMUNICATION
FRIENDSHIPS
Page 113
Page 162
BIG SCHOOL
Page 106
HUMOR
PUBERTY
Page 178
COLLEGE
SPECIAL INTERESTS
Page 204
Page 50

Welcome to Abigail's World. The handy map on the previous pages should give you an idea of the places we'll be visiting during this book, along with the freedom to explore at a pace that suits you.

Want to take a trip to **BIG SCHOOL**?
Skip to page 162.

Feel like a short stop-off for some **FOOD**?
Turn to page 96.

Need a **BATHROOM** break?

Well, there are plenty of toilets dotted around, so that shouldn't be a problem. Plus, you can just put the book down anytime and "go." I'm fine with that.

Now, you might have noticed there was already a contents page at the front of the book in a **nicely organized list**. Well, I'd like to think of this book as more of a map.

A map of my mind.
Grouped by theme and
linked by my memories.

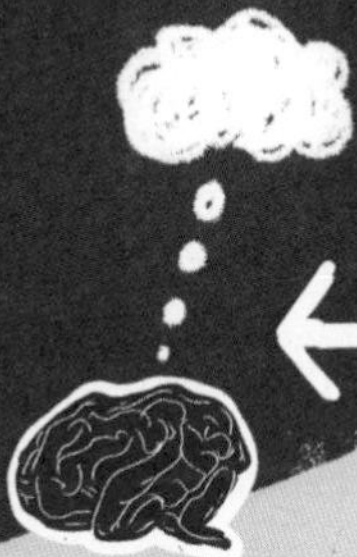

A collection of my
thoughts and experiences,
which don't always follow
a strict chronological
order or a neat structure.

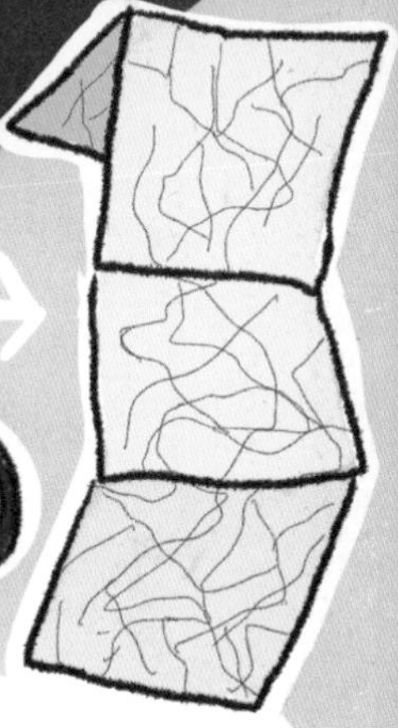

In fact, perhaps you could even think of this book as a conversation. A really rambling, slightly one-sided one, but a conversation nonetheless. If you'd like me to slow down or you want a chance to process my words and pictures, simply take a break and pop back when you're ready.
I'll still be here.

Now, instead of starting at the beginning, let's start at a place you are probably quite familiar with . . .

SCHOOL

You know how old people sometimes say patronizing things, like

> The kids these days don't know they're born!

AND

> The school years are the best years of your life!

Well, firstly, I have always known I was born (stupid phrase). I'm reminded of it every year, with an awkward celebration where we count how many years it has been since I was born and where everybody sings a song about it **AND** for some reason they all **CLAP** loudly afterward. (Are they clapping for their singing or my birthday?! Both feel ridiculous to me.) Then we eat miniature versions of regular food, which is mostly beige, and I have to pretend to like balloons because my dad's friend has decided to spend half an hour blowing one up even though they are actually, basically the **WORST** objects ever, because:

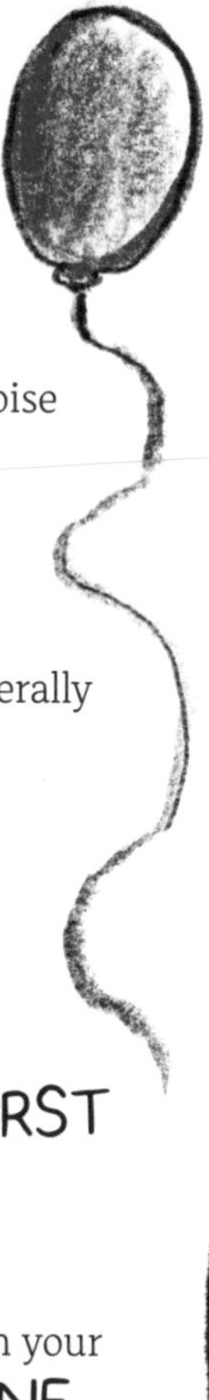

A) if they pop, they make a **HORRIBLE** loud noise

B) the texture makes my veins shudder

C) they **KILL** poor defenseless animals and generally ruin the environment

?? WHAT'S THE POINT?!

Secondly, my school years were definitely the **WORST** years of my life.

So if you're hiding in the soundproof music room on your lunch break right now, trying to avoid **EVERYONE** (I am speaking from experience), or if you're at home dreading going to school tomorrow because the effort of trying to appear "normal" is weighing heavily on you (also speaking from experience), let these words be a small bit of relief for you:

it DOES get better.

YES, REALLY, IT DOES.

I think those adult people who say

> I wish I could go back to childhood, when things were a lot simpler.

have obviously never:

1. been bullied for being different

2. fallen down the stairs on the way to French class (in a skirt!!)

3. been called **"Wednesday"** every day (not just on Wednesdays) because they were pale and had dark hair and a serious face

4. experienced many other **NOT** good things that are definitely also **NOT "simple"**

The above all apply to me by the way, in case you didn't realize, but then you probably **did** realize because I have already told you that this is my **TRUE** story, which is a little bit scary to be writing down **again** because it makes it even more **REAL**.

But, also, it's actually quite nice to be opening up about these things to you, dear reader, because in a way we're becoming friends and getting to know each other like friends do.

Anyway. Where was I?

Oh yes . . .

So please don't worry if your school years are **not** the best years of your life either. It's entirely possible that the best years of your life are yet to come . . . Until then, what better way to pass the time than to hear about someone else's not-very-normal experience of school (i.e., mine)?

BUCKLE UP. And put your backpack on. **And** make sure you've brushed your teeth and had your breakfast—but **NOT** in that order. (So many things to remember on a daily basis, I know.)

LET'S GO TO SCHOOL . . . (Well, not **actual** school. We're going to stay inside the pages of this book for now, thankfully.) Here are some of my first memories from elementary school:

Being scared to use the bathroom

Making a girl cry by kissing her

Making a boy happy by kissing him

Two older girls fighting for my attention in the playground (No one my own age seemed to want to fight over me, though.)

Let's explore that first one in more detail, shall we? But first, I must warn you now, if you haven't already noticed, I can sometimes ramble a bit. (OK, a lot.) I tell my stories as things pop into my head and I don't always seem to have a filter or a neat way to organize my thoughts before they come out.

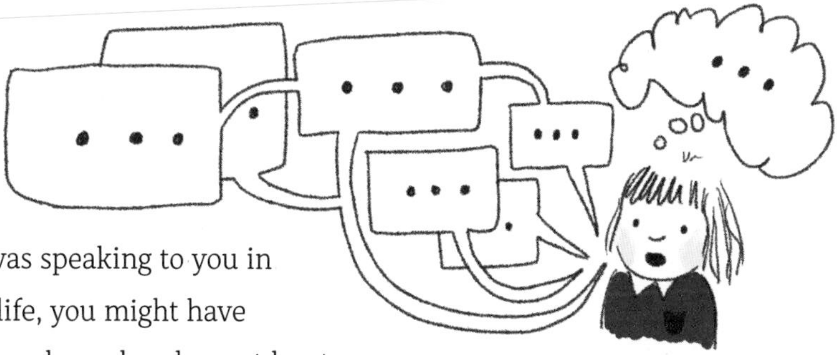

If I was speaking to you in real life, you might have fallen asleep already or at least asked me to STICK TO THE POINT. But luckily, as I am **writing** this, I am able to go back and delete words and put them in a good order. Or an order that I like the shape of anyway. But that doesn't mean I won't still ramble a bit.

So . . . why am I telling you this now? Good question. I almost forgot myself, but the answer is this: I have SO many stories and memories and thoughts to tell you, and they are not all easily told in one sentence or one picture, so I'm going to have to be selective about which ones I include. We don't want this book to be so big that you can't fit it in your school bag or so heavy that you can't hold a cup of juice and a **cookie**[5] at the same time as you carry it to your room, do we?

Right. I'm glad we've had this discussion. I'll get back to writing about my life then.

TOILETS!

Am I REALLY going to start this fresh new chapter by talking about my bathroom habits?!

OK, yes—YES, I am.

My earliest memory of elementary school is:

My earliest memory of high school is:

And, yes, you guessed it, my most **recent** memory of school involves toilets too.

5. A packet of cookies.

SO TAKE A SEAT.

(On the toilet, perhaps, or on a chair—there are no rules here. You can even stand up if you like.)

I suppose you could call toilets my **NUMBER-ONE** topic. So **URINE** trouble if you don't like wee (or wee-wee) stories. And by "wee" stories, I mean small stories. **YES**, that was, in fact, a **TRIPLE** pun. Who says autistic people don't have a sense of humor?! (OK. The last one was a **lie**[6]. My stories are anything but "wee.")

Toilets basically ruled my whole school experience. Not because I needed to use them all the time, but because I refused to use them at all. I wouldn't use them at break times. I wouldn't use them at lunchtime. And I certainly wouldn't put my hand up in front of the class to ask to use them.

6. Autistic people generally find it difficult to lie, hence why I followed up my lie with the truth. I'll get to that in a bit.

One day, when I was five years old, I came home from school and headed straight to the bathroom. My dad, noticing my urgency, asked me when I had last been.

"This morning." I answered with **the facts**.

"At recess?" he questioned.

My dad's face dropped. Which means his face **CHANGED IN AN ANGRY WAY**.

His face did not fall on the floor. Or in the toilet. Thank God. (If you believe in Him/Her/Them. I usually thank "Goodness," whoever that is.)

Yes. Dad was **MAD**. Even I, a five-year-old autistic child, could see that. He was one not-happy father. Even his eyebrows looked angry. In fact, **especially** his eyebrows . . .

Dad's ANGRY eyebrows

Dad's not-angry eyebrows

My dad demanded I tell him why I hadn't used the bathrooms at school. But I'm not sure I actually **knew** why. Apart from the fact that I had a **paralyzing FEAR** of using them. I knew I didn't **want** to use the school bathrooms, but I didn't know how to tell anyone about the overwhelming feelings that had led to me avoiding them.

He made me promise to use the school bathrooms tomorrow.

I PROMISED.

But the next day I didn't use the school bathroom.

After school, my dad checked in on my bladder-emptying activities.

I remembered how angry he had been the day before, so I lied and told him I had used the bathroom at lunchtime. I knew lying was bad. It didn't feel right. It made me feel sick to my stomach. But I also knew that the alternative was being shouted at, which felt much, much worse.

It was easier for me to pretend to be normal, someone who could use a public bathroom just like every other **child**[7] at my school, than it was to be faced with an Angry Adult Person.

FACT:

Many autistic children are very honest. Telling the truth is often a natural instinct, which can sometimes make us seem blunt or uncaring.

7. I don't actually know if every other child could use the bathrooms at school, though. I think there is a high chance that other kids like me were crossing their legs the whole day. While I was writing this book, my editor told me he was also too scared to use the bathrooms at school for many years. Facts.

However, we are usually anything **BUT** uncaring. Though we sometimes learn that saying things we don't mean can help us to fit in with certain groups, and at times it can make our families and friends feel better. This is not crafty or deceptive in any way. It comes from a place of longing to fit in, a place of aching to be loved and accepted . . . a place of wanting to make those closest to us happy.

My dad just wanted me to have a healthy bladder, after all. And I just wanted him to achieve that wish.

So, anyway, this toilet situation was something that continued long into my teens . . .

Looking back now, I'm pretty sure my public bathroom fear started from a combination of the below.

- Disgusting smells
- Dirty seats
- Fear of being locked in
- Fear of not being locked in and someone walking in
- Tracing-paper toilet paper that didn't absorb anything
- Weirdness of taking underwear down at school
- Not knowing what was happening outside the bathroom door while I was inside. Were people laughing at me? Ready to play a trick on me?
- The large, loud, cold, echoey school bathroom building, which hundreds of children had to use

And then, when I actually **tried** to use the bathroom, something unfortunate always seemed to happen . . .

Location: AZTEC MUSEUM
Age: 9

I attempted to use the bathroom on a school trip but forgot how to pee, then I lost the rest of my class for long enough to put me off using the bathroom on any sort of trip **EVER** again.

Location: BIG-SCHOOL BATHROOMS
Age: 14

I stuck a handwashing poster up in the girls' bathroom because I'd noticed several people not washing their hands when leaving the stalls. People wrote swear words on it, ripped it up, and made fun of me in my yearbook a couple of years later.

Location: MOVIE THEATER
Age: 28

I got locked in a movie theater overnight because I fell asleep on the toilet. It took me hours to escape from the venue. The next day my girlfriend went back to the cinema to search for the cardigan I'd left behind. While she was there, the manager, who recognized her from the security footage, had questions . . .

Anyway, all this toilet talk has made me need to go to the bathroom. Yes, I am going to stand up, walk to the bathroom, and use the toilet right now. I might even leave the door open.

RIGHT! It's time for a non-toilet break. This is all getting a bit too toilet-y for my liking. And we all know I do NOT like toilets.

SPECIAL INTERESTS

I can get fixated on things. That much is probably already obvious. Once I've found a subject of choice, I run with it, much to everybody else's dismay, amusement, or delight. (Who knows what other people are thinking, really—we'll get on to that later.)

At various points in my life these have been some of my favorite things to talk about and obsess over.

My Little Ponies, Littlest Pet Shop toys, Pogs

I preferred to play alone with my toys so I could make up the rules.

Key rings

I collected hundreds of them before I owned even a single key.

Spice Girls

My room was covered in posters, and I recorded every TV show they ever appeared on.

Crystals and their meanings/uses

So pretty AND so useful.

Star signs

I like to predict people's star signs—tell me about yourself and I bet I can predict yours!

Hamsters

I drew hamsters on all my schoolwork and cried many tears when my pet hamsters died.

Poop

When I was fourteen and first discovered the internet, I made my own (very basic) website called **Let's Talk About Poop**, and I emailed it to my forty-something-year-old half brother, who I hadn't spoken to since I was four years old. I don't think he was as amused by it as I had hoped he would be.

Learning and reciting the capital cities of South America

Anytime a South American country was mentioned at school, college, or anywhere at all, I immediately called out the capital city. I still do now.

Winning the Geography Prize in Year 10 even though I had never traveled outside the UK

I was proud and surprised, and I still bring it up regularly.

Saxophones

I was obsessed with the idea of playing the saxophone when I was fourteen and saved up my pocket money for a LONG time to buy one.

Weather

I repeatedly check the weather app on my phone throughout the day and enjoy seeing what the weather is like in different parts of the world.

My FAVORITE *EastEnders* (UK soap opera!) episode ever

I was so obsessed with the dramatic Valentine's Day episode of 1999 that I designed a denim school bag based on the plot using cuttings from soap magazines.

Apparently autistic girls' special interests are likely to be "normal" interests that lots of "normal"girls like, such as

music and makeup and cute animals, but they will often be interested in a more intense or specific way. Whereas autistic boys' special interests tend to be those which are thought of as "classic autistic" special interests, such as trains or timetables or numbers.

FIRSTLY, just writing that makes me cringe because it incorrectly squishes everyone into two genders in such a binary way. People who believe that gender is "binary" assume that there are only two genders: men and women, boys and girls. But as we know from my diagram earlier, gender and gender expression are actually a lot more fluid than that, kind of like a tub of ice cream that started off frozen but is now loosening up after it's been left out of the freezer[8] for ten minutes.

8. This seems like the ideal moment to tell you about the time my dad took a tub of ice cream back to the supermarket because it had melted. He was very disappointed with the gloopy liquid mess, but luckily the supermarket person allowed him to exchange his faulty ice cream for a new tub. But a day later my dad was back at the supermarket after encountering the same problem with his frozen dessert. "I've had it up to here

That might just be the worst metaphor I have ever created, but I am not a metaphor expert. In fact, I'm not an expert on any of the things I am writing about (well, apart from myself), but there are some really excellent experts out there if you're interested in learning more about any of the things that I bring up in these pages. I've added a few to the back of this book (including the term "gender-fluid")!

SECONDLY, I've definitely displayed a combination of both so-called **girl** and **boy** interests. While my love of the Spice Girls may not have raised any questions or eyebrows, my obsession with the number

22

is such an autistic cliché!

with this ice cream!" he shouted. The startled supermarket person inspected his tub and, sure enough, it had melted. She issued my dad a refund. It was at this point in my dad's story that I decided to ask him a very important question. "Dad . . . Where had you been storing your ice cream?" My father paused. "In the cupboard," he said . . . with absolutely no hint of sarcasm whatsoever. THE END.

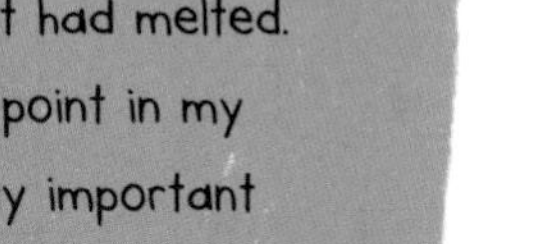

Special interests for autistic people can look different across genders, but it's also important to know that they can look different across **people**. Everyone is different, and our likes and dislikes can't be squished into the narrow categories of "boy" or "girl."

I have always loved monologuing (talking at length) on my favorite subjects, but I didn't know why until very recently. Now I understand that when I monologue I'm practicing the autistic art of **infodumping**.

INFODUMPING

Infodumping, common among autistic people, involves giving an extremely detailed summary of a favorite topic in a single heap.

Although it can feel amazing to infodump on people, while at school I became increasingly aware that not everyone liked my long rambles on unusual subjects.

But LISTEN UP! (Yes, I'm talking to you again, dear reader-friend-person.) It's **healthy** to have special interests. It's **healthy** to be passionate about your favorite things. And it's **healthy** to expend your energy in a way that feels physically and emotionally good to you—as long as you are safe and not causing anyone harm in the process.

Enthusiasm and fascination are powerful and magnetic, and no one should ever make you feel bad for loving what you love. The greatest inventions and pieces of art and music were born from intense special interests and an unwillingness to give up, even when surrounded by people with opposite views or those who were reluctant to champion their dreams.

And that's pretty special. And very interesting, I'd say.

Even today I can sometimes find it difficult to work out whether someone is enjoying it when I ramble about my favorite topics . . .

EMOTIONS

People are complicated. Their thoughts and emotions and likes and dislikes do not fit into neat boxes, despite what surveys and feedback forms might have us believe.

Just look at social media and the emoji. Emojis are either happy or sad or confused. They are never a mixture of all three. (Unless you use all three, which is entirely possible and lots of people do.)

But that's not how people's faces work. Oh no, you can't ask someone to clone themselves for each emotion they feel **and** use the appropriate face for each emotion when you speak to them. You have to work out their reaction in that moment, while listening to their words **and** dealing with your surroundings. That's **a lot** of multitasking.

REAL FACES ARE COMPLEX.

Yet, saying all of this, I often find myself not only **understanding** what someone in front of me is feeling, but actually **feeling** their emotion too. (I might, however, not be able to follow the words they are saying if I force myself to look them in the eye at the same time, so there's a chance I'll be looking at the wall behind them instead!)

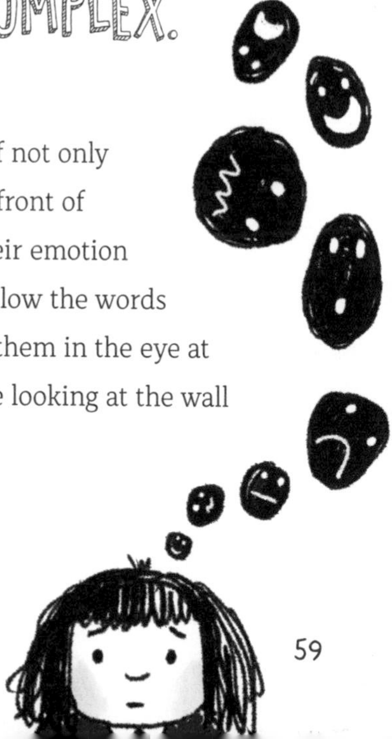

MYTH: Autistic people lack empathy, i.e., the ability to understand what someone is feeling.

FACT: Autistic people are often extremely empathetic, and can even absorb the emotions of those around them due to sensory sensitivities.

Like many autistic people, I am an empath. Although I sometimes find it difficult to identify my own emotions, I feel other people's moods, emotions, and energy on a deep level. I will often absorb the feelings of whoever I am with.

I don't have a **huge** problem reading faces either, perhaps because I am extremely sensitive to energy—and I am an illustrator so I have studied facial expressions a lot! But many autistic people do have trouble reading faces. See, the so-called common autistic traits are not always clear-cut.

When I was fifteen, my family actually thought I was **lacking** emotion due to my "choice" of special interests. Apparently my urge to write and draw certain dark subjects suggested to the people around me that I did not feel emotion. But, ironically, hearing people say this made me feel extremely hurt—clear proof of emotion!

HERE ARE SOME THINGS THAT HAVE MADE ME CRY WITH EMOTION

- Being misunderstood by friends and family who thought I didn't have any feelings

- A very soft sweater—I didn't realize it was possible to find clothing this soft and I loved it so much

- Pinocchio and Bambi and The Lion King and some other sad movies

- Realizing I couldn't save all the animals in the world—a very sad day

- Being stressed at school

- Being stressed at work

- Being pushed off a chair by someone I thought was my friend

- My best friend not wanting to be my best friend anymore

- Seeing a happy baby

- Someone bringing me flowers

- Missing dead relatives

- Seeing a really delicious-looking cake on a dessert menu

- Visualizing getting a book deal, imagining it was true, and making some tears of gratitude happen

Most of these tears happened while I was alone or with one very trusted person. You see . . . just because I am not always openly **displaying** an emotion, doesn't mean I'm not **feeling** an emotion. Plus, there are other ways to process emotions that don't involve crying. For example, some autistic people flap their hands and jump around a lot when they are happy or excited. I have tried that and can thoroughly recommend it. Rolling around on the floor is pretty fun too. Yes, it can get you some weird looks, sure, but as long as you're not hurting anyone, who cares?!

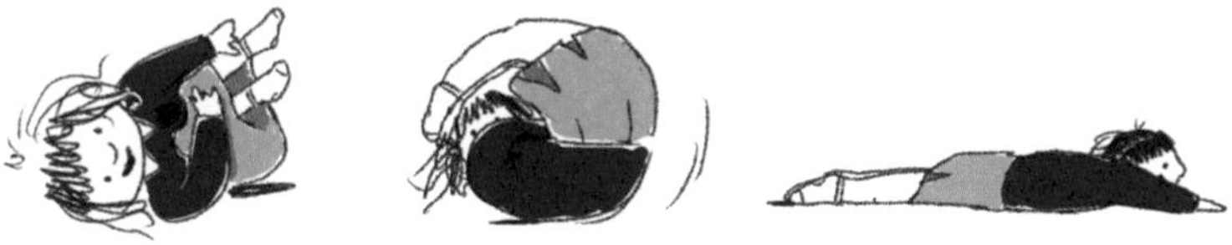

For some reason, there seems to be an allistic desire for us to perform emotions in a specific way for the comfort of allistic people. This is harmful and ableist.

ABLEISM

The discrimination against disabled and neurodivergent people based on the belief that typical abilities are preferable.

Now, although I am very sensitive to the moods of others, I do sometimes find it difficult to understand and **identify** my own emotions. If someone asks me how I'm feeling and they actually want an answer that isn't

then it can take me a while to work out the answer. And when I find myself in an emotionally stressful situation I won't always react in a **"normal"** way—how people around me expect me to react. I might need time on my own to process a situation, for instance.

But, really, what is a "normal" way to react emotionally to life? We are all made up of different pasts, presents, and futures; we have different likes, dislikes, and levels of comfort. There is no right or wrong way to "feel" or to show that feeling to others.

You are **allowed** to just be who you are, without judgment.

And that includes judgment of yourself.

Because often we can be our own worst critics.

FAMILY

Since I briefly mentioned my family in that last chapter, now seems like the ideal time to formally introduce you to them.

MEET MY FAMILY.

Families are funny if you think about it. You suddenly find yourself within one when you are born, then you usually have to live with them for several years until you are old enough to live on your own. Some of us begin life with blood-relative families, some with adopted families, and others with foster families or carers.

Some people will say this family tree was just an excuse for me to show off that I am related to a very important composer. And they would be right. Listen to his "Bohemian Girl" overture on Spotify. Even Queen Victoria was a fan. Famous.

We are all shaped by the people we spend time with, whether by learning their behaviors, absorbing their energy, or automatically being born with some of the same genes as our parents and siblings.

For me, it's definitely a mix of all three.

FACT: Autism can run in families. Children with an autistic sibling or parent have nine times the usual odds of being autistic, and children who have a sibling or parent with a brain condition other than autism have up to 4.7 times the usual odds of being **autistic**[9].

Although I didn't **think** autism ran in my family, it's looking more and more likely that it does. My mother, who is now sixty-six years old, is currently on the waiting list for an autism assessment. It was only through my research and diagnosis that we started to see our similarities. When my mom desperately tried to "improve" things for me, like encouraging me to be social (and to enjoy parties) when she herself found it difficult, she simply wanted me to have an easier life than she did.

9. According to research published in the *National Library of Medicine*. In reality it's likely these figures under-represent the real odds since many autistic people are diagnosed in adulthood or never get diagnosed at all.

AND THERE'S MORE . . .

I'm pretty sure my nana was autistic too **and** she had Alzheimer's—one of those brain conditions I mentioned before. I wouldn't be surprised if her mom and her nana were autistic too.

And then there's my brother, Patrick. I'm pretty sure he is neurodivergent. Patrick is hilarious and unusual and talented and in my opinion fits a lot of the criteria for ADHD—and some of autism too.

Perhaps that's why we got on so well as children, with our obscure senses of humor and our love of winding our mom up by doing the strangest things, such as printing out a picture of her face and sticking it inside the microwave with sticky tape.

I found my brother so entertaining that I used to write down every vaguely amusing thing he said to me and my mom. The next day I would then take those scraps of paper to school in my pencil case and recite them to whoever was sitting next to me in class.

While other teenagers in my class were talking about who they had crushes on and their favorite pop stars, I was reading family stories to people who had never met my family. (And at this point they were probably hoping they never would!)

I found Patrick in my room whispering in the cat's ear. He was asking her to tell him her innermost thoughts, but she got up and walked away.

Even though my home life wasn't without its issues, it was familiar and it was what I felt most comfortable talking about, so it became one of my special interests. In fact, it still is. I have been known to read full chapters of my dad's autobiography at dinner with friends, and no partner is ever safe from my collection of family videos.

Family is part of me. Part of my life and my memories. There is no such thing as a "normal" family, and I'm proud to be part of our small and ever-so-slightly unusual one.

Dad and Nan are no longer alive, but their love still remains in my heart.

Sometimes it can feel like there are lots of parts of life to cope with all at once. Add to that demands from the immediate surroundings and we suddenly have a lot more to deal with . . .

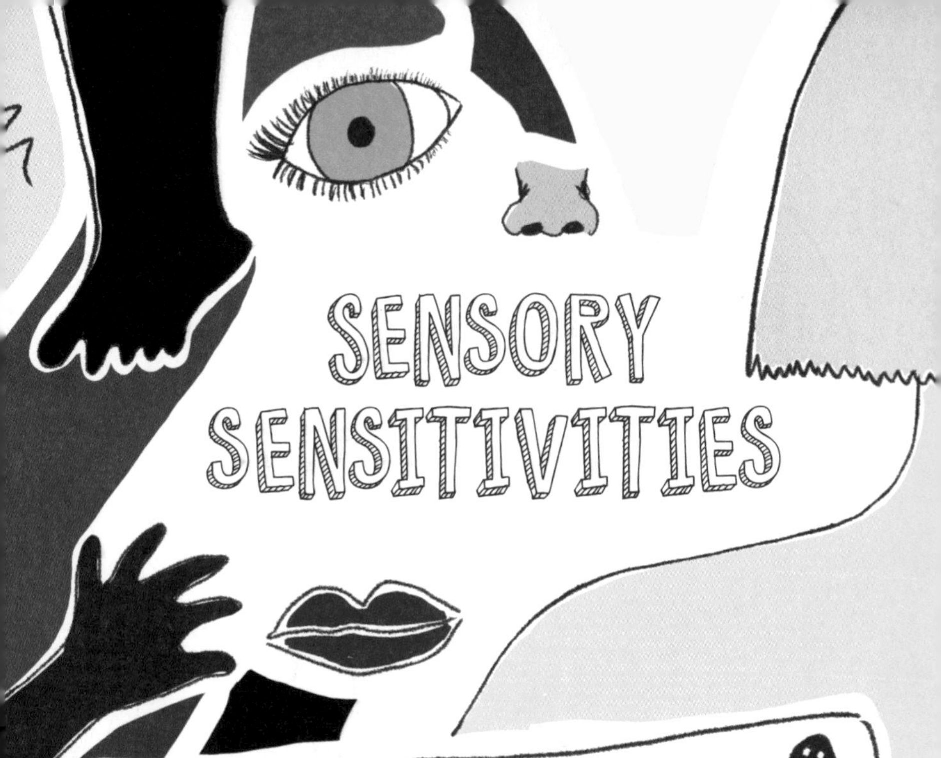

SENSORY SENSITIVITIES

ENVIRONMENT

This does not just mean green fields and forests and oceans (i.e., that big important place we live in that needs saving urgently). When talking about autism and sensory stuff, the "environment" means everything around you: the things you can see, hear, smell, taste, and touch, and the people you find yourself around.

Sometimes I feel like I need an extra layer of skin between me and the outside world. I experience everything very intensely. Sounds, emotions, energy, lighting, pain. Often it's possible to deal with these one at a time, but a combination can prove very challenging.

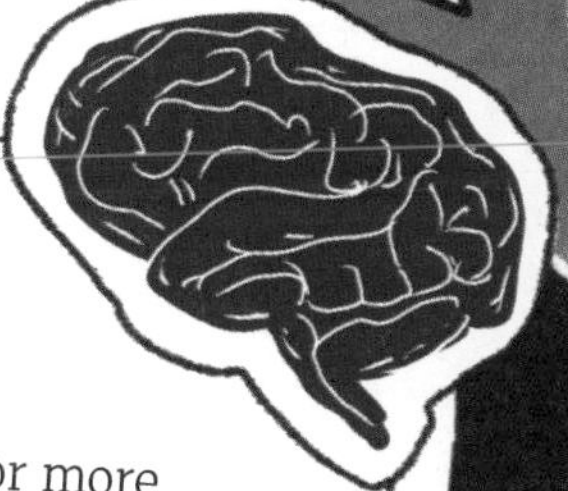

SENSORY OVERLOAD

Sensory overload takes place when one or more of the body's five senses experiences too much stimulation from the environment and the body doesn't know how to process it. Sensory overload can be triggered by a crowded room, fluorescent lighting, a TV turned up too loud, strong smells, and many other things. Anyone can experience it but it's commonly associated with autism.

I am writing this chapter on the train.

This is one situation that causes my senses to become overloaded, and I figured that would help me get the words to feel **REAL**.

HERE WE GO . . .

MONDAY: 9:43 a.m.

LONDON COMMUTER TRAIN

Journey time 22 minutes.

(My favorite number, thank GOODNESS, or this would be a whole lot worse.)

Let me paint a picture. But with words—I simply cannot paint while I'm on the train because multitasking is not my thing.

A baby has started crying. The fluorescent lighting is too bright for the early daylight hour and what is the point when this is a train with **windows**?!

The overhead announcement repeats the same words it repeats every day, which no one is listening to.

A sniff. A jingle of keys. The squeak of sneakers, the rustle of a newspaper.

A carrier bag, a rain jacket. It hasn't rained for days.

And someone STINKS. Not just a small whiff of unwashed hair, but a nose-hair-yanking FOUL stench that makes me gag and immediately feel terrible because that poor person might not be well or happy.

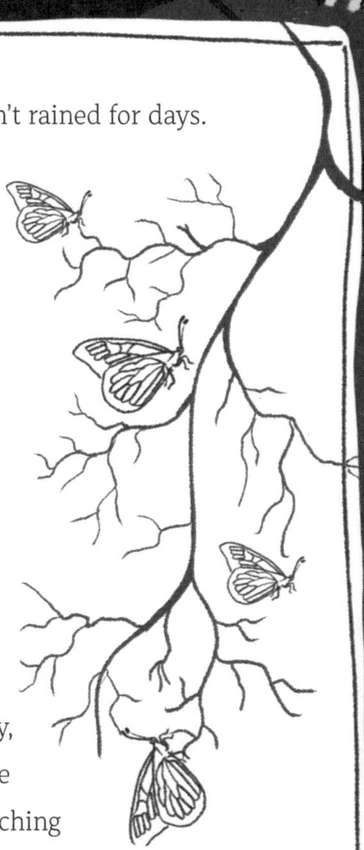

I feel sensory overload as both a physical and an emotional[10] thing. My veins get sore and itchy. My head feels swollen, dizzy, and full. And my chest flutters like the family of moths I've been watching eat all the clothes in my wardrobe for the past five years.

I keep these feelings inside, exit the train, leave the platform, and start walking toward my office, ready to begin a full day at work.

10. My editor asked me to include the emotions I was feeling, but that's just the thing—in the moment of sensory overload I am unable to identify these emotions. I can write down the physical sensations in my body, which are all tied up with emotions, but labeling those exact emotions is trickier.

I'm writing from home again now in the quiet. (And I drew the pictures on the previous pages while at home too. Obviously.)

Similarly, when I'm in a social situation, I know I have a limited time before the demands of the environment become too much for me . . . After a while, everything starts to feel LOUDER and BRIGHTER and more intense than it did when I arrived. And the time it takes for this to happen entirely depends on:

1. the nature of the environment
2. who I am with and what is expected of me while I am there
3. how I am feeling that day

I find it much easier to socialize in wide-open and quiet spaces, such as parks, beaches, and forests, than in busy and noisy pubs, restaurants, or shopping centers. And I much prefer meeting up with a friend for a one-to-one chat than I do meeting up with a group of friends. Equally, if I am feeling stressed or haven't had enough sleep or food that day, I'll find a social event harder to cope with. Generally I am able to manage around two hours at a gathering before I feel the need to leave. Sometimes this will be more, sometimes less.

It's funny to think that up until a couple of years ago I wasn't fully aware of all this. I would push myself into uncomfortable situations to please other people, which resulted in the **worst anxiety** both before and during events,

followed by **complete relief** when I was finally home alone, recovering. I would feel sad that I couldn't seem to enjoy the things that "normal" people enjoyed, or do "normal" things, like go to school or work or leave the house to go shopping, without feeling sick to my stomach.

If you've ever had to sit in a classroom with children talking over each other, fluorescent lights, and teachers shouting demands at you, then you'll know that sensory overload and the anxiety it creates feels **a lot** worse than looking at a lineup of colorful cats.

I painted these cats because I love cats and I thought that **MAYBE** if I drew the cats creating the sensory issues I might not feel **quite** so anxious.

It sort of worked. Because I like looking at the cats.

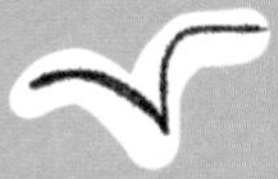

One place I was always safe from sensory overload as a child was my nana's backyard. Her house backed up to some woods and a field of horses, and at the bottom of her yard sat a huge swing. I would hop from stone to stone, careful not to touch the surrounding grass, as I made my way toward it.

My nana was a big kid herself and did a lot of research and planning to find a swing that was perfect for adults and children. I would grasp the thick ropes and push myself off the ground with my feet, soaring high above the houses.

I loved the rhythmic feeling of swinging

back

and

forth,

back

and

forth,

the vast space around me, and the houses below bobbing up and down. It was as if I was *actually* flying and nothing could touch me up there. I felt invincible.

During my school years, I used this time on my nana's swing to imagine all the fun and amazing things I would do with my life. I hadn't heard of visualization (creating pictures of things in my mind) at that point, but I knew it felt good to picture the brilliant and joyful things that were possible in life.

One thing I remember feeling particularly excited about was going to "the baths," as my nana called the swimming pool at our local rec center. My friend from school was having a birthday party there, and I was thrilled to have

been invited. The idea of doing something **"fun"** that "normal" children did was an extremely attractive prospect to me. I remember repeating in my head

while on the swing and feeling very grown-up and "normal."

My mom, however, was worried, seeing as:

1. I'd never set foot inside a swimming pool before

2. the idea of driving me there filled her with dread. Autistic adults + driving to new places

= 

3. I couldn't swim. Not. One. Bit.

Plus, my mom couldn't swim either, and my dad wouldn't have been caught **dead**[11] in a public pool.

When the party day finally arrived, I wasn't quite as excited and brave as I had been at the dizzying heights of my nana's garden swing. I wasn't creating the perfect day in my mind anymore; I was out in the actual real world—exposed and naive.

As I soon realized, the swimming pool involved a whole lot of new things to worry about and consider: the unfamiliar smell of the chlorine-soaked building, getting changed in front of people from school, trying not to get lost, TOILETS (yeah, I know . . . wish me luck!!), the fluorescent lights overhead, the loud, echoey room where I was unable to hear anything anybody said to me or to each other, and deep water (which I was in both literally and metaphorically).

11. He certainly wouldn't have been caught alive in one either. I'm not too sure why being caught DEAD somewhere is an example people use. I don't think many people would want to be caught dead in most places, including places they like.

The screams of my classmates having "fun" were particularly grating on my ears and my nerves, especially after the lifeguard (who I don't think deserved such an important title) picked up a hose and pelted me with water.

I IMMEDIATELY WENT UNDER.

I couldn't breathe.

I couldn't see.

I couldn't scream for help.

Luckily one of my friends noticed I was in danger and came to my rescue, pulling me out of the water to safety. I actually don't know what would have happened if she hadn't helped me—I definitely couldn't have helped myself.

Why had no one else noticed though? Why was the lifeguard . . . smiling? Were the other children smiling too? Why could no one see I was struggling, even after I had been rescued?

If I could tell when a person was sad or happy or angry, why couldn't anyone in the pool apart from that one friend see that I was not OK?

Looking back now, I realize no one could sense my discomfort, probably because sensory overload was not something they could relate to. Plus, I did not react verbally (speaking out loud), as an allistic child might have done, by screaming or shouting. My facial expression probably remained the same throughout the experience too.

This awareness of being **"different"** from other children was an all-too-familiar feeling . . . a feeling of being overwhelmed by my surroundings but unable to verbalize it—unable to say it out loud.

From puppet shows to pool parties to school discos and events—I still put myself through all of these because that's what I thought I "should" be doing. **Ha!**

If only I knew what I know now: I am in charge of my own life, and my comfort and safety are worth prioritizing. I don't need to force myself into boxes, trying to fit some sort of "normal" child-shaped mold. I don't need to put up with loud, busy, overwhelming situations. As long as my choices don't cause harm to myself or to anyone around me, I should be free to make the choices that are right for me.

Sometimes I still find it difficult to leave situations when I've had enough, but I am learning and making progress. If I'm somewhere anxiety-inducing and it's impossible to leave, I usually find myself stimming and not able to form sentences properly.

STIMMING

A self-soothing behavior that is marked by a repetitive action, sound, or movement of the body (such as tapping on objects, snapping fingers, blinking, rocking from side to side, grunting, singing). It is typically associated with autism.

MY STIMMING LOOKS A BIT LIKE THIS:

rubbing thumbnail

tapping and rubbing lip

Other more extreme reactions to sensory overload look different for different people. It might seem like the person is having a panic attack, it might appear like they are shutting down, or it might look like they are having a tantrum.

FACT: The two main responses to sensory overload are a **MELTDOWN** or a **SHUTDOWN**.

A meltdown can often look like a tantrum. But it's important to understand that it is definitely **not** a tantrum. A tantrum is usually aimed at gaining some sort of reaction or response and may stop after the child gets what they want. A meltdown is a natural reaction to stress, the environment, and/or to demands being placed on the person.

A shutdown is what I experience. I can't speak, and my face doesn't know how to make the right shapes anymore. Unfortunately, to other people, it just looks like I'm not interested in the conversation. (Actually, there's probably a good chance I'm not, but that's beside the point.) I feel detached from everything, like I'm watching a scene on a TV show, yet at the same time I'm trapped **inside** the TV.

Once, when I was nine years old and at a parents' night, my teacher told my mom that I was very hardworking, but it was as if I had blinders on (like a horse wears). I appeared to be focused on my work but wasn't looking at, or reacting to, anything going on around me. I now realize that was because I was regularly surrounded by sensory overload triggers. I **had** to block out everything in that overwhelming classroom situation—I **had** to mentally remove myself because there was nowhere I could physically run off to.

These moments kind of sum up my inability to respond during sensory overload and sensory anxiety. I am often not able to speak out at the time, but after space alone to reflect, and once I have my voice back, I can write down my thoughts or try to explain what's happened.

Unfortunately shutdowns can be mistaken for avoidance behavior or rudeness . . .

. . . when **actually** shutdowns are a natural automatic response to stress and are often triggered by sensory overload.

If I am experiencing sensory overload, I often need to leave the situation immediately to lie down in a quiet environment alone.

But due to people's expectations and how I'm feeling at the time, it can be difficult to make that positive choice for myself. Not only is it considered rude to get up and walk off during lunch with friends or an important class (this needs to change!), but it's also hard to immediately communicate my needs to other people, or even to know what those needs are.

(Cats don't have this problem. **Cats are lucky**.)

However, since my diagnosis I've been learning new ways to cope with everyday life things, such as giving myself a time limit for social events, turning up early to settle into new environments, and choosing a seat or table in the quietest spot. The better you know yourself and your limits, the more natural-feeling (or "normal") being in this strange human world will become!

Maybe autistic children and adults could have access to something like a set of cards they can pass to whoever they are with before they stand up and silently leave. I made some here that you can trace or photocopy, or you could even make your own. (Do schools still have photocopiers? I'm not sure, but if they do, now is the ideal time to use one.)

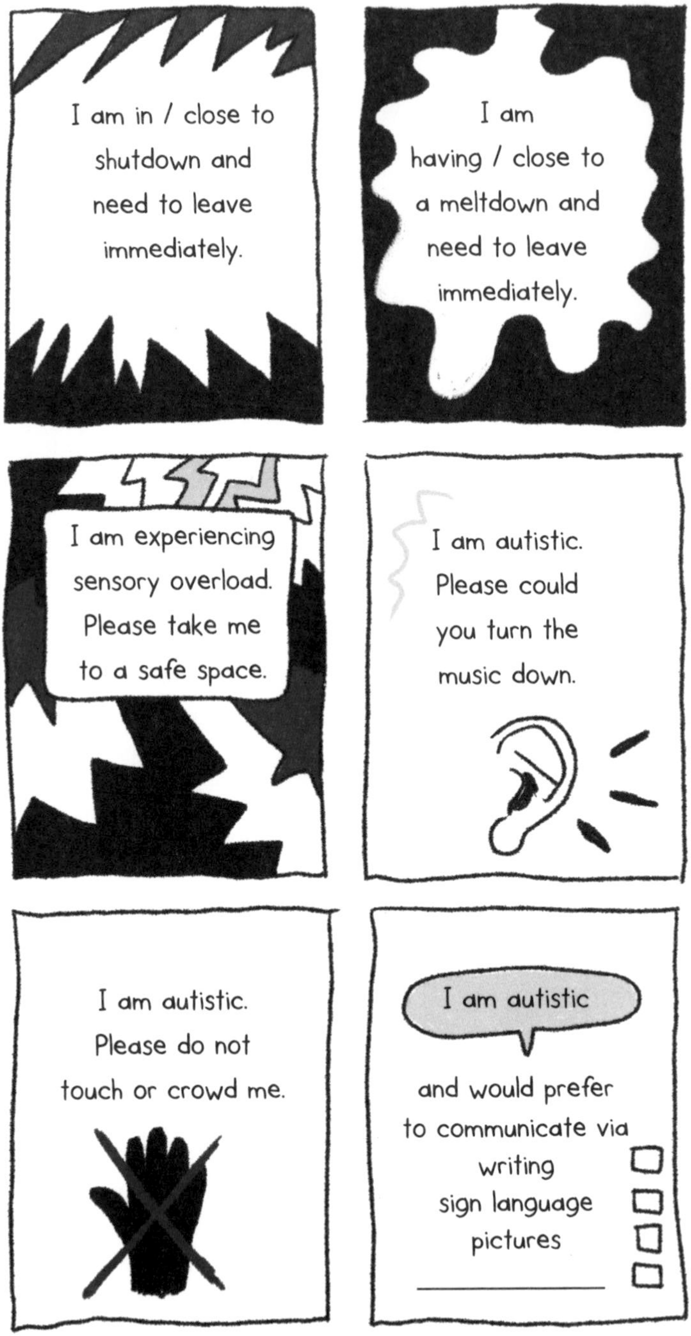
I am in / close to shutdown and need to leave immediately.
I am having / close to a meltdown and need to leave immediately.
I am experiencing sensory overload. Please take me to a safe space.
I am autistic. Please could you turn the music down.
I am autistic. Please do not touch or crowd me.
I am autistic
and would prefer to communicate via
writing
sign language
pictures

HOW TO HELP SOMEONE EXPERIENCING SENSORY OVERLOAD

This is important for those of you who maybe don't experience sensory overload yourselves but know someone who does.

DO

- ✓ Remove as many of the sensory stimuli (the things causing the sensory overload) as possible
- ✓ Stand guard for them while they cover their ears and close their eyes to block out the stimuli
- ✓ Give them space to just "be" and stim away to their heart's content
- ✓ If possible, offer to accompany them to a safe place, away from whatever has caused the sensory overload

- ✓ Allow them to communicate with you non-verbally if they wish to. This might involve giving them a piece of paper and a pen, your phone to type on if they find that easier, or asking yes/no questions that they can nod or shake their head to

DO NOT

- ✗ Touch or crowd them
- ✗ Ask them open-ended questions (a question that can't be answered with a "yes," "no," or other short response)
- ✗ Place demands on them
- ✗ React negatively to their overload/shutdown/meltdown

But, guess what? Sensory sensitivities can also be a nice thing!

Let me tell you about some of

MY FAVORITE SENSORY THINGS

- Everything soft

- Soft blankets. I have around seven on my bed at any one time and like to feel gently weighed down by them. One day I will invest in a weighted blanket.

- The insides of very soft clothing

- Rubbing a scratchy bit of my thumb on my lip. I do this when I'm nervous or thinking. When I was a child, my mom would come home from her night shift as a nurse and I would grab her thumb and say, "Scratchy thumb" and rub it on my lip. It's soothing and my version of stimming—I didn't know that word even applied to me until I was diagnosed.

- Soft lighting. I love salt lamps and fairy lights. I have a calming color-changing aroma diffuser that looks and smells relaxing.

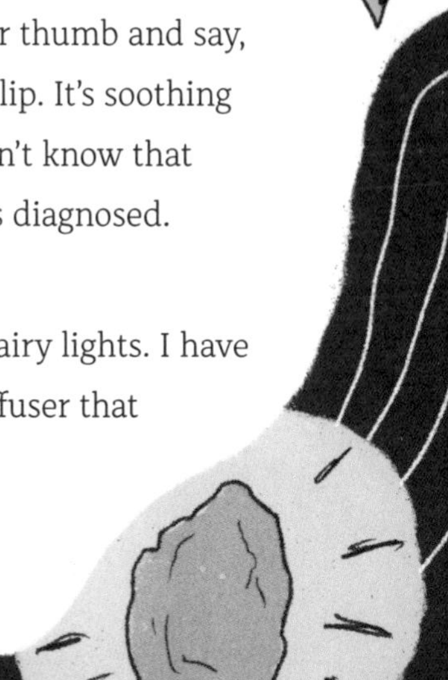

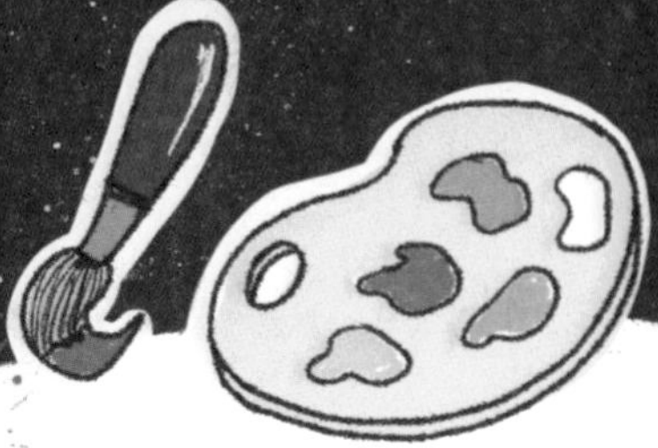

- Pleasing color combinations. I love staring at my favorite colors and mixing them in my paint palette.

- Mashed potatoes, soup, and gravy—all the soft food groups

- Certain perfumes, shampoos, soaps, candles, incense, etc. These are things I will keep going back to sniff. I can't get enough of some smells. As I type this, I am furiously sniffing the air in my room because of the leftover smell of incense. It's better than you could imagine it to be and frankly I'm sorry you can't experience it for yourself. Well, unless you buy Om by the Mother's India Fragrances. This is not an ad.

SOCIAL COMMUNICATION

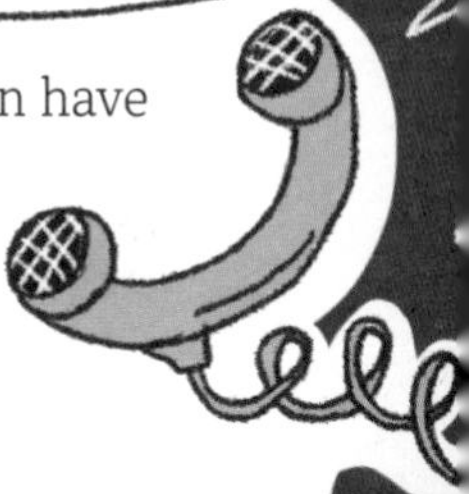

All children develop at different rates. And all children have different ways of seeing the world.

For autistic children, those differences may be more noticeable in some areas than others.

In order to receive an autism diagnosis, a person has to demonstrate having lifelong difficulties with these three areas:

- **SOCIAL COMMUNICATION**—struggling with verbal and non-verbal language, including tone of voice, eye contact, body language
- **SOCIAL INTERACTION**—finding it hard to start conversations, responding to others, and keeping a conversation going
- **SOCIAL IMAGINATION**—finding it difficult to imagine what others are thinking or to make changes to their own routines. (Not to be confused with creative imagination!)

Although I spoke out loud from an early age, I'd say my use of language and the sounds my voice made were quite unusual compared to the people around me.

Sometimes I sounded posh . . .

Sometimes I sounded French . . .

And other times I sounded like a forty-year-old teacher with a child's voice . . .

Even though I disliked school, I would come home and convince my brother to act out classroom scenes with me, where I was the teacher and he was the student. We would record ourselves and listen back to the tapes, laughing at the parts where Patrick said something funny. I loved pretending to be someone else—someone older, someone respected, and someone in charge. Slipping into character for an hour or so would take me away from my insecurities, my awkwardness, and my uncertainty about my place in the world.

My use of the written word wasn't exactly "normal" either . . .

Miss Henderson wasn't quite so splendid a few months later when she shouted at me for coloring outside the lines. I was five years old! (And heartbroken.)

In moments of extreme stress and sensory overload, I find it difficult—sometimes impossible—to speak out loud. This is known as selective mutism, and it is extremely common within the autistic community.

SELECTIVE MUTISM

An anxiety disorder where a person is unable to speak in certain situations, such as in a classroom or around relatives they might not know very well.

However, I like to call it **situational** mutism, because "selective" makes it sound like a choice. It is definitely **NOT** a choice. For me, it's a physical reaction to stressful things in the environment (my "situation") and it means my face stops knowing what to do with itself.

I know from speaking with autistic friends that others experience it this way too. Some autistics call this **"going non-speaking"** or **"going non-verbal."**

Some of the ways I have communicated with humans while alive in this strange, neurotypically designed world:

- Followed children around the playground staring at them and not talking because I didn't know how to start a conversation

- Recited stories to classmates to try to get friends

- Was chosen to represent my school in a public-speaking competition because I was good at reading out loud
- Emailed my boyfriend of nine months to split up with him instead of speaking to him face to face, because I knew the words wouldn't know how to come out in real life
- Managed to avoid answering the office phone for over three years by always wearing headphones

How I feel about some of the ways I have communicated with humans while alive in this strange, neurotypically designed world:

- PHONE CONVERSATIONS: SCARY. Difficult to know when it's my turn to talk. I have to prepare a script before phoning people, even my friends.

- EMAILS: a good form of communication, but it can take some time to construct the perfect email

- INSTANT MESSAGES: I like the more casual nature of these and that I can add emojis to emphasize my point. But I can also get overwhelmed and avoid my messages for days. Things like blue ticks, "read" receipts, and the "ONLINE" feature make me nervous, but these can often be changed in the settings!

- **SOCIAL MEDIA:** I get paid actual money to work in social media, so I am very good at this. I love meeting new people on Instagram in particular. I have met some amazing people in the autistic community this way, and I would like to meet even more!

- **FACE-TO-FACE CONVERSATIONS:** with one person at a time, these can be amazing and special and fun. With more than one person, they can be an overwhelming assault on the senses.

I think one of the most unusual ways I've used to communicate with people is the method I am about to tell you now . . .

When I was sixteen and had to start a new school, I knew I had to think of something inventive in order to make friends. Friendships were not something that had come easily to me, and they were becoming more difficult as I grew older. Luckily I had the perfect idea. Using scraps I had left over from Home Ec, I cut fabric into tiny pieces, and then I wrote "POO" (the way we say "poop" in the UK) on each one. I proceeded to laminate each piece of fabric, which involved wrapping it in Scotch tape and making sure each edge was neat and straight with a pair of scissors. I probably had about a hundred in total. (I needed to make sure I wouldn't run out.) I placed my collection of poo (poos?) in a transparent makeup bag and put it into my backpack.

I was the first to class that day in early September. PERFECT. I sat in view of the door, in the second row (well, I didn't want to look TOO eager), and I waited for the students to start to arrive. As each new person entered the classroom, I stood up and said, "Hello! Would you like a lucky poo?" while offering up my bag of poo.

I had my twelve-word script memorized to perfection.

The structured conversation I had planned for each person made me feel confident and in control of my surroundings. In control of myself.

When someone accepted a lucky poo, I would casually introduce myself.

The responses flowed effortlessly. What a huge change this was from the school I'd known before! I was **taking control** of this scary new first day at school—opening up conversations and making people feel . . . er . . . well, I was going to say "at ease," but some did look a bit . . . nervous, perhaps? That was fine, though. At least it wasn't **ME** looking nervous for a change.

Sometimes we just need to find the most comfortable way to communicate **for ourselves**, and then we'll attract like-minded people (and animals) to communicate with us in this way.

Tues Sept 4, 2021
Offered everyone in my class a lucky poo.
Lots of people accepted.
One person wanted two.
My tutor even wanted one AND a boy even stuck one on his guitar!

As an autistic person, I often feel like everyone knows something I don't. Like they're all in on a really funny joke that I just can't understand or find the point of. Which is ironic, because apparently quite a few **people**[12] suspected I was autistic before I did.

Autistic people often have an "unusual" sense of humor . . . Though, actually, it's only unusual if you compare it with the allistic sense of humor and assume **that** sense of humor to be normal—which I don't!

12. My brother, my ex-boyfriend and his friends, and a girl at a party. There are probably a few more people who have asked me if I'm autistic, but this has only happened from the age of twenty onward. No one suspected a thing when I was a quiet, well-behaved child getting on with my homework and keeping out of trouble.

I prefer **my** sense of humor. I'll often be found laughing at jokes no one else finds funny, and I might not understand the jokes that everyone else is rolling around on the floor laughing at (rotfl).

My sense of humor has been described using the following adjectives:

I used to do stand-up comedy in my late twenties and it was a very enjoyable experience. People sitting in chairs forced to listen to me monologue about my life? PERFECT!

Though sometimes the audience members didn't always laugh in the correct places and that would distract me from my very excellent stories. I would tell them off for not laughing in the space I had planned for them while struggling to remember my next line. Thankfully this made them laugh even more!

Which brings me to another thing: sometimes autistic people (including me) can laugh at "inappropriate" moments, so I decided to put the following list together to help myself, and potentially you too.

A LIST OF THINGS NOT TO LAUGH AT

- **SOMEONE WHO FALLS OVER,** especially an old person or a child or a pregnant person. In fact, laughing at **anyone** who falls over is **NOT** very kind. **So** . . . why then are there television programs made up of lots of clips of people falling over with an actual laugh track to encourage the audience to cackle?! This does not make **SENSE**, does it?!

- **AT FUNERALS OR AT PEOPLE TALKING ABOUT FUNERALS.** Yes, death can sometimes be funny (for example, when my dad asked me to scatter his ashes in an ashtray at his local pub), but generally death is regarded as A Sad Event and people don't take kindly to others chuckling at it. However, funny things can happen where death is concerned, like when dead bodies **FART**.

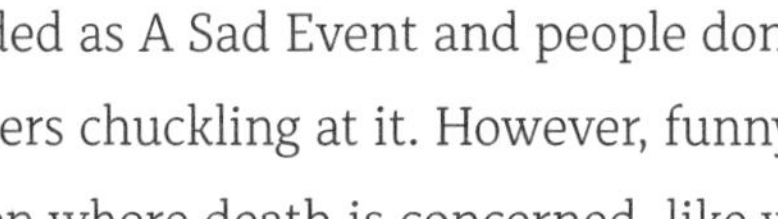

- **SOMEONE WHO IS UPSET OR CRYING.** It might seem obvious, but humans generally prefer a reaction that is appropriate to the situation. If someone is sad, you can try to make them laugh, but laughing *at* them is not a good idea.

- **WHEN SOMEONE TELLS YOU SOMETHING SERIOUS WITH A SERIOUS FACE OR A SERIOUS TONE OF VOICE.** This could be a piece of bad news or sad news. Again, people expect your face to match their face at a time like this. Although a lot of autistics can be good at mirroring (reflecting) the behavior and expressions of other people, sometimes the intensity of a situation can bring about an "inappropriate" reaction.

Also, humans generally expect the same from you if **you** are the one telling them something serious. For example, most people don't know how to react when I tell them that my dad is dead and then I laugh. I'd be happy for them to laugh with me to ease the seriousness of the topic, even though I love my dad and it would be a lot more fun if he was alive and telling me stories.

- **TRAGIC EVENTS IN HISTORY OR THE NEWS.** Sometimes the ridiculousness of news events might be laughable, but laughter should be used sparingly.

Now, you **may** wonder why I'm telling you not to laugh at some things that are just really obviously not a laughing matter, especially since we recently discussed how empathetic and sensitive autistic people can be. Well, sometimes our physical reactions to situations aren't based on our actual feelings about those situations. We might get so overwhelmed by someone telling us their cat died that a laugh comes out by mistake, before we are able to offer words of sympathy. This doesn't make us uncaring or any less human. If anything, it shows our worry and anxiety about responding "appropriately" in order to make that person feel OK.

Just like ~~selective~~ situational mutism, and just like meltdowns and shutdowns, we are simply reacting to our environments. It's OK to not always get it "right" (in the eyes of an allistic person) the first time. There is no "normal" way to be in this world. If your heart is in the right place, then that's all that really matters, I think.

FRIENDSHIPS

MYTH: Autistic people don't want or need friends.

FACT: Some autistic people may not be particularly social, but many crave human connection and are more than capable of being amazing friends.

Yes, there are many **asocial** autistic people out there (those who take little enjoyment from socializing)—my mom being one of them! But there are also autistic people who value friendship highly. Often, however, we can find it difficult to make those friends and to maintain those relationships due to our social communication issues and different ways of experiencing the world.

Plus, interacting with other people can be **exhausting** and sometimes we might feel that our energy is better reserved for the things we need and truly **want** to do, such as arranging our collection of erasers by color or planning how to save all the giant otters in the world.

I'm not speaking from experience on those last two examples, but here are some actual real-life things that I found a lot easier than making friends when I was at school:

- Writing long essays
- Playing "Moonlight Sonata" on the piano
- Hiding from my brother for a very long time in a hedge in the garden without him finding me

- Spending quality time with my cat
- Drawing pictures of Victorians, nineteenth-century boats, and hamsters wearing vests

✓ Eating seven packets of chips in one sitting. (I bought a huge box of out-of-date chips from a yard sale. I figured it would make sense to eat them quickly because no one likes soft, chewy limited-edition curry-flavored Hula Hoops, do they?)

Things that **didn't** make the above list because I didn't find them easier than making friends include:

- ✗ Fractions and other complicated math puzzles
- ✗ Speaking out loud in class without my voice wobbling
- ✗ School discos
- ✗ PE class
- ✗ Thinking about PE class

So, yes, friendships made it somewhere on the

- "confusing, yet I want them"

section of my list of

- "Things that are apparently supposed to happen in life."

I even made a couple of imaginary friends in my room using pillows, clothes, and patio chairs when I was about nine years old, because they were easier to be around than real humans.

When I was younger, the rules of friendship seemed to change without warning.

One of my earliest memories of friendship is sitting next to a girl called Sally[13] in elementary school. I'm assuming that's how we became friends—because we were placed next to each other. Do you remember how, when you were five years old, you could be friends with almost **anybody**? Maybe you had a friend when you were five who suddenly no longer talked to you and you weren't sure why. Well, let me tell you, I have been there. And it's confusing.

My friend Sally and I did everything together—which basically involved sitting in class and playing on the playground. I remember we wrote

"I love you"
and
"You're my best friend"

in each other's school books when we were six.

13. Her name wasn't Sally, but apparently changing the names of real people in books is important these days. I am a real writer now. Yayyy!

She also came to my birthday parties, something that I remember made me feel particularly proud. She and other people from school actually wanted to come to my **house**!

So I felt very confused and left out when I saw her playing with another girl on the playground one day.

I attempted to join in, and although I wasn't excluded as such, I just couldn't understand how another friendship had formed without me noticing. Where was I when these two had decided they would become friends? Why had I not noticed? Was I not **enough** for her?

OK, so it might sound a bit **dramatic**, but changeable childhood friendships were not something I understood or felt particularly at ease with. I was always one step behind—watching, second-guessing myself, and hoping I was getting it right.

A pattern started to emerge throughout my school life. As soon as I developed what I thought was a strong friendship, another girl would come along and appear to be better friends with that person almost instantly. Now, I may not always **understand** everything about social interaction, but I have an excellent eye and ear for detail[14], and I could see from the girls' body language and hear from their inside jokes that they had **definitely** been hanging out at each other's houses after school.

WITHOUT ME.

Of course, I didn't mention this. Because that would have been weird, right?

Or would it?

14. In fact, I have two excellent eyes and two excellent ears.

I'm still not sure what the "right" and "not right" (i.e., wrong) ways of reacting to things are. And who decides what is right or wrong anyway? Can't everyone just decide what **feels** right for themselves? Unless they're into animal cruelty, of course. In that case they should definitely **NOT** be deciding what is right for themselves—or for anyone else for that matter. And **especially** not what is right for the animals. They should also definitely totally be arrested or told off in an appropriate way.

Anyway . . .

Yes.

THE GIFT OF AN ANIMAL FRIEND

Sometimes I feel like I get along better with animals than with humans.

A cat can provide hours of fun.

And a cat will always let you know when it's had enough.

You don't expect a cat to show the correct facial expression or share the same excitement as you about something.

Yet a cat still knows when you are sad and will be right next to you with a helping paw . . .

For a bit anyway.

THE BEST THINGS ABOUT CATS

- They are grateful for the simple things in life, such as food, water, and snuggles.
- They don't expect me to talk when I look at them, and they are happy to just sit quietly and be in the moment with me.
- They meow if they have something to say, but they don't meow for the sake of filling silence.
- They confidently leave a situation if they've had enough of being social, so I don't have to worry that they don't want to be around me anymore.
- They are very soft. I like soft things.

In some ways a cat can provide a much simpler friendship than a human can, so it makes sense that I really like cats.

Now I'm going to draw a whole page of cats just because I want to. Yes, it really is that easy to make a decision to do something you love because it **FEELS GOOD** and won't harm anyone.

I think I just got distracted talking about cat friends instead of human friends, but that's because cat friends are so good. However, human friends can also be really good, though admittedly they're not always quite as straightforward!

Some of my favorite human friends[15]:

JENNY

When we were in middle school, Jenny and I decided that one day we would open a Really Amazing Business together. We both liked art and writing and animals, and spent our weekends renting films from the video shop, rewinding the funniest parts again and again, laughing until cola dripped out of our noses. I really enjoyed

15. I have changed some names of people who might not want to be included on a shelf in a bookshop.

having a loud, confident friend because I was not loud or confident, so I clung to her throughout middle school until I moved away. We tried to maintain our friendship by writing letters and calling each other on our house phones. This was before the internet and cell phones so it was extra hard to keep in touch.

Apparently that last fact means I'm kind of old too. But I certainly don't believe that, as I still feel like my age is permanently twelve. I've also been told many times that I don't "look" my age either. In fact, when I was thirty I was mistaken for my partner's **child** while passing through airport security. My partner was younger than me too, so she was **not** amused.

Autistic people can often appear younger than allistic people, not just in terms of behavior but sometimes physical appearance too. There are lots of theories about the reason for this. Is it because our faces are often less expressive than allistic faces, and so we aren't creating laughter and frown lines as quickly?! Is it because our body language and mannerisms are different from allistic people's? Or is it because some autistic people have an above-average **skull size**[16]?!

16. According to the US National Library of Medicine, head circumference (measuring the head all the way around) could be used as an early predictor of autistic traits in younger siblings of autistic children.

Maybe it's a combination of reasons and perhaps it's not relevant to all autistic people, but either way—I find it quite interesting!

Now, where was I?

Oh yes . . . Jenny.

So anyway. I realized only recently that after we got back in touch as adults that I am now no longer on her Facebook friends list. Did Jenny simply remove the people she no longer talks to? Or had I done something to upset her? Did I post something insensitive online? Or were my previous messages too overly familiar when we hadn't spoken for years?!

BUT THAT'S JUST THE THING:

sometimes there **isn't** anything we have done. There might also be nothing we can do to bring that friendship back—and nor should we. Sometimes friendships meet natural ends, and I truly believe that's to clear the way for better, healthier relationships to enter our lives.

People change and it wouldn't be right if we stayed with the same friendship groups for our whole lives. Imagine if you ran out of information on your favorite special subject to tell your friends about?!

That said, I do know people who are still best friends with the friends they made when they were five, and that works wonderfully for them. Happily, I now have friends who I have lots of things in common with, and some of them are even autistic too!

SARAH

We met when I was four years old. Sarah's family lived at the bottom of a hill and I was always scared my mom would crash the car on the way down the hill because it was so steep. This does not tell you about Sarah, I know, but my dislike of steep hills is something you should know because I don't want to do a book signing at the top of a hill or at the bottom of one, so I'm hoping my publisher is taking note of this section. Many thanks in advance.

EMMA

She was my best friend when I was sixteen and one of the first people to accept a lucky poo. We sat next to each other in music, and the teacher told our parents we were attention seekers and should sit apart. Emma was openly gay, which was something I really admired at the time since I was not. She worked part-time with disabled children and used to ask if she could hold my hand using sign language when we were on the bus.

LOTTE

I found Lotte in the kitchen hanging out with my roommate during my first week at college, when I was twenty. She was odd, like me, but neither of us realized at the time that we were neurodivergent. While I was autistic, Lotte was dyslexic and dyspraxic. I often get on really well with people who are dyslexic. Our brains work in interesting and unusual ways and when we get together something magical happens. Lotte and I are still good friends today, fifteen years later.

MIRA AND MAR

We were in a band together when I was twenty-five. They are funny and nice and easy to be around. I used to hate staying away from home overnight when I was younger, but I went on tour in Germany with Mira and Mar for over a whole week **twice** and I really enjoyed it. We used to have this saying:

A band that poops together stays together.

Well, unfortunately I didn't ever manage to use the toilet next to them, so perhaps that's why we split up in the end? We are still good friends ten years later, even though we live in different cities and countries.

BIMPE, CHRIS, AND DEE

We met at work when I was twenty-seven, and each of us looked after the social media accounts of some very famous music acts. We laughed a lot, despite being busy and quite stressed most of the time. We all ended up leaving to pursue new careers, and we championed each other's choices. We still speak regularly on WhatsApp and in actual REAL LIFE when we meet up for lunch and lols.

I'm very sorry to the friends I didn't include on my list; there is a word limit to this book and strangely I seem to have more friends than I thought I had, which is really quite nice to realize.

As you may have noticed, my best friendships actually happened later in life. There is no **"normal"** pace to collect and build friendships, so if you're struggling right now to connect with anyone, if you are lonely, or if you are desperate to meet someone who gets you on your level, believe me—it really is possible.

And hopefully if this is the case for you as it has been for me, it will be such a relief and so joyful that you will be glad you didn't have such good friendships when you were younger, because only now are you able to appreciate the magic of these really excellent ones.

One of my favorite things to do when developing a new friendship is to work out that person's birth chart. I have found astrology to be something that I can use to really see into human behavior and emotions, and it's helped me understand why people act and react the way they do. It might not be for everyone, but it's one of my favorite special interests so I must tell you about it while you are here!

BIRTH CHART

A birth chart is a map of where all the planets were at the time of your birth, and how this may affect the way you live your life.

SUN—your main personality/identity sign and the core of who you are

MOON—rules your emotions and represents your inner self

MERCURY—determines how you communicate, think, and process information

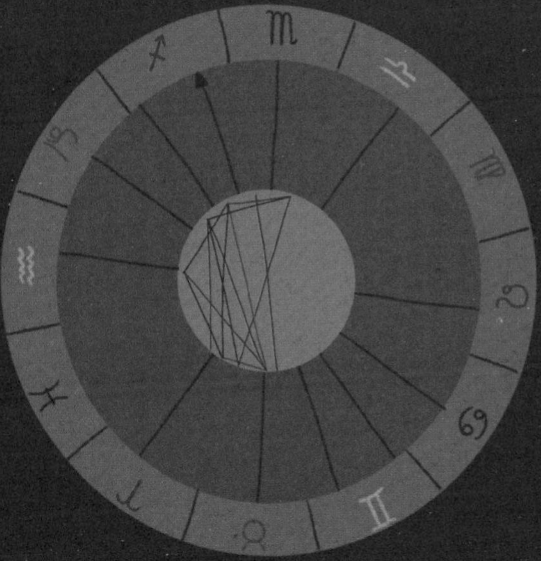

VENUS—dictates how and what you love; how you express affection

MARS—influences how you assert yourself and take action, and is the energy that surrounds you

ASCENDANT (rising) sign—the "mask" you present to the world. (Yes, it's not just autistic people who mask!) This sign represents how you appear to other people when you first meet them.

My nana had a collection of huge astrology books hidden at the back of her wardrobe. Anytime I visited her and mentioned something that had happened with a friend from school, Nan would ask me for their date of birth before digging into her thick encyclopedic book collection. She would then tell me what astrology said about that person, how compatible we were, and why they might behave the way they do. My nana even went to college in her sixties to study astrology.

As I said earlier, I'm pretty sure my nana was autistic. She was actually obsessed with having friends. Each Christmas she would write a list of which friends had sent her Christmas cards and proudly recite it to me and my mom, comparing the number with last year's total while commiserating that certain cards must have been lost in the mail because she had **definitely** seen that person in the village buying a newspaper only a few days ago, so they were **also definitely** still alive.

My mom and I silently wondered (and then out-loud wondered when we went home) how she'd managed to collect so many friends over the years when we could count the number of friends we had on one hand. OK, yes, she was old, but if you think about it, a high percentage of her friends would probably have been dead by then, so I was quite impressed that her list didn't seem to get smaller over the years. Maybe that was because she was starting to add people like "John the computer man" (he fixed her computer) and "John the rust" (he fixed the rust on her car). Imagine making such an impression on a car mechanic thirty years your junior that he sent you a Christmas card? She was quite the character.

But, yes, my mom and I found it a lot harder to jump on board the friendship train. (I'm not sure why I keep using trains to illustrate my point.)

See, different things take different amounts of effort, time, and energy for different people. And we all have different priorities in life. We can't all be talented artists while also solving the world's hunger problem. We can't all be talented athletes while also saving the giant otters (but, if you're interested, you could search "HOW TO SAVE THE GIANT OTTER" because, as I've recently discovered, they really do need our help). And we can't all be really amazing musicians while also being experts at making enough friends to hold a pool party at the local rec center. Because, well, the world would be a bit boring if everyone could do **everything**, wouldn't it?

BULLYING

Unfortunately, the title above jumped into this chapter without me asking it to. It sort of crept up on me while I was writing about friendships.

I didn't ever fully realize that I was being bullied when I was at school, because I had a few friends and I didn't ever get spat on or anything. But on reflection I guess I must have been.

The thing about autism is that we don't always have insight into our own experience. We can be very good at watching, listening, and helping others, but when it comes to our own "place" in the world and how we relate to other people, things can get a little blurry.

When I was at school, for me the word **"bullying"** conjured up pictures of that loner kid being beaten up by the bike rack for their lunch money, because that's the kind of bullying I saw on TV.

Nobody did that to me, though. I always managed to walk home without being jumped on, I never left the bathroom with a bloody nose, and I don't even know if our school **had** a bike rack.

Yet I felt extremely unsafe and exposed while on school premises, as well as on my journey to and from school . . . It was as if I was waiting for someone to suddenly point out the strangeness of my existence, to grab my arm and hold it high, shouting to the world,

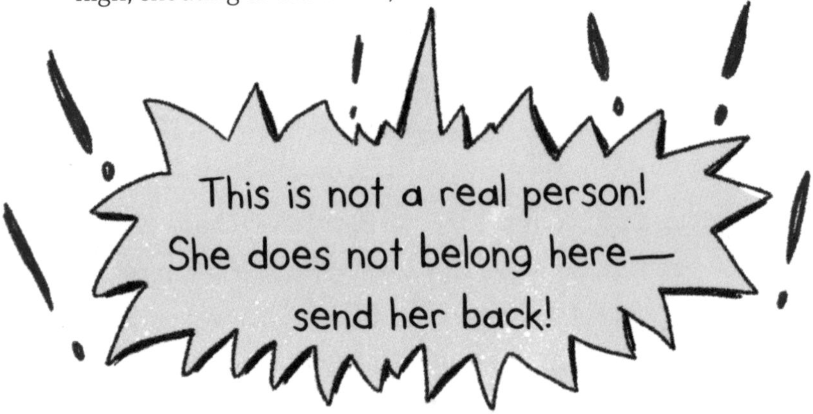

Of course that never happened. At least not in so many words.

But here are just a few experiences from my school years that I can **now** see meant I was, in fact, being bullied and I really should have done something about it. Not even "should," I **deserved** to have something done about it.

1. My first voicemail message on my first-ever cell phone.

2.

This might seem like a genuine question but it was actually someone making fun of me for having my gym uniform in two shopping bags. Her face had a disgusted look on it.

So I ignored her.

3. The day I snapped. (Well, as much as a polite, quiet, well-behaved girl could snap.)

After lunch one day, I walked to the classroom to find the boys had barricaded the door with tables and were refusing to let me in. They told me to climb over the tables, so not knowing what else to do I climbed onto a table. They proceeded to shake it until I fell off.

I'd had enough. I was exhausted from trying to "be normal," which clearly was not working. I had not done anything to these boys. I was just being ME.

As the anger rose inside of me, I leaped on one of the boys and grabbed hold of his hair, pulling it as hard as I could (which wasn't very hard, luckily). He was shocked, as were my classmates, who all stared in silence. After a few seconds I let go of him and went back to my seat.

I'm not proud of how I reacted in that moment, but I'd been pushed to my limit.

I don't think the bullying stopped. And I don't think the teachers ever found out. Because I didn't tell anyone. And neither did anyone in my class.

To me, what I was going through didn't feel significant enough. I found talking of any kind challenging, so I wasn't going to start a conversation on a difficult subject with an adult when I couldn't be sure that I really needed to. I didn't trust my own judgment. I didn't think I was being bullied "properly" or "enough." (I know, how ridiculous does that sound?!) So I just left it. I put up with it.

Occasionally I saw other kids being picked on too and decided it was just part of life. When, really, I should have stood up for them—and for myself too.

I'm going to conclude these bullying stories by saying something that is probably completely obvious to you already: bullying is NOT OK. In fact, bullying is one of the most horrible things you can do to a person. It is much nicer and much kinder to be . . . well, kind and nice. And, at the same time, it's important to acknowledge that people who bully are not necessarily "bad" people. They will have their own issues and problems that need to be worked through. We never know what's going on in someone else's head or in someone else's life. But what I do know now from my experience of bullying is that being hurt by another human does not feel good. It sticks with you.

HERE'S THE GOOD NEWS, THOUGH:

One day it **did** get better for me. And if you are being bullied right now, one day it will get better for you too. Sure, it can take some work to learn how to protect yourself from bullying, but freedom from bullying really is possible.

You won't always be at school. Or college. Or the same job. Life is constantly changing and adapting, which can actually be an extremely refreshing and freeing thing. **Yes**, even for an autistic person like me who doesn't like change!

WHAT TO DO IF SOMEONE YOU KNOW IS BEING BULLIED

- **Tell an adult**, e.g., a teacher or parent
- **Be with that person** and support them, e.g., walk with them to school or class
- **Reassure** the person that it's not their fault
- **Ignore the bully** and shift focus to the person being bullied—don't be tempted to fight back as that's likely to make the situation worse
- **Encourage others** to support the person being bullied
- **Confront the bully**—only if it feels safe to do so—by verbally asking them to stop

BACK TO SCHOOL

Suddenly this has all become quite serious! But sometimes it's important to have serious conversations. Because life isn't always just about toilet jokes. And it would be a bit poopy if it was.

Let's take a step back for a minute, shall we (but check there's no one behind you first), and remember where we are. The answer to this almost-question is probably **"school."**

Even if you're at home or on the bus or in the park right at this moment, the likelihood that you will have to go to school at some point over the next few days or weeks is high, mainly because this book can be found in the eight-to-twelve-year-olds section of your local bookstore.

Books have to be categorized by age groups, you see, even though this book is actually for people of all ages. I like categories, don't get me wrong—they can help us place things and make sense of the world in easy, manageable **chunks**[17]. But they can also be a bit limiting.

If I'd stuck to eight-to-twelve books when I was eight to twelve, I would have probably felt very frustrated and bored. I also wouldn't have learned about the more grown-up world of high school, dating, and relationships.

Even though it felt like a lifetime away for me then, it was actually pretty good preparation for my developing mind. We'll revisit this in a few pages' time (or you can skip to page 178 if you can't wait), but for now . . .

Let's go back to school.

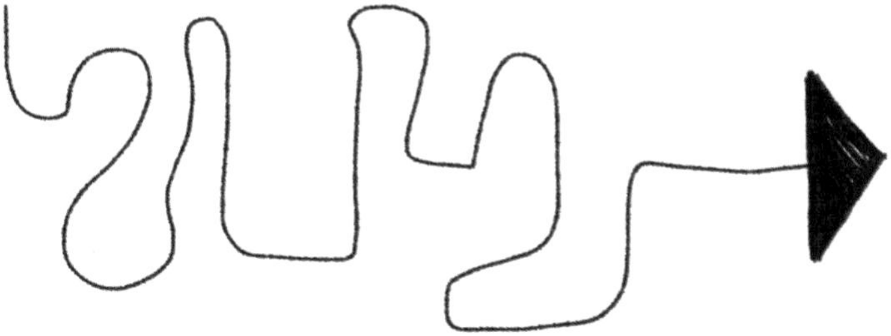

17. I don't like the word "chunks." It reminds me of both vomit and cat food. I suppose cat food is the better of these two because at least it involves a cat. I should have chosen an alternative word, but then I wouldn't have been able to tell you my thoughts on this particular word. I do hope it was worth it.

Throughout my school life I was a quiet, well-behaved child. I kept my head down and got on with my work.

My report cards were always impressive and parents' night was always a cause for celebration, as the teachers predictably told my mother that I was

a joy to teach

and

top of the class.

My only so-called negative feedback was that I should

contribute more to class discussions.

Yeah, like I wouldn't have already tried that if I could've physically opened my mouth and made actual sentences come out without gaps and stuttering! I **was** a complete nerd in every other way, after all . . .

In fact, I put so much pressure on myself to "achieve" and to receive this positive feedback from my teachers and parents that schoolwork took over my life.

Although I was academically intelligent, I did not thrive in the classroom. Actually, I found it extremely painful in multiple ways.

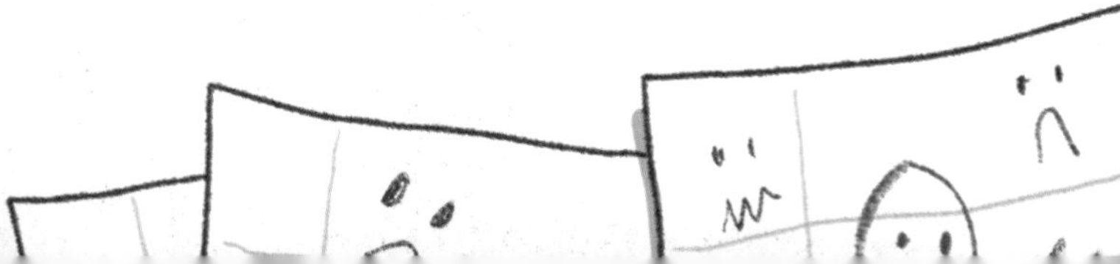

CLASSROOM
NEW TIMETABLE
SENSORY OVERLOAD ALERT
To Do
• Study
• Eat/drink
• Avoid toilet
• Avoid bullies
• Avoid speaking in class
• Get friends
CAMPUS MAP
N
S

Now get into groups of four and—
TICK TOCK
TICK TOCK
IMPORTANT TESTS
DEADLINES
MORE DEADLINES
HOMEWORK

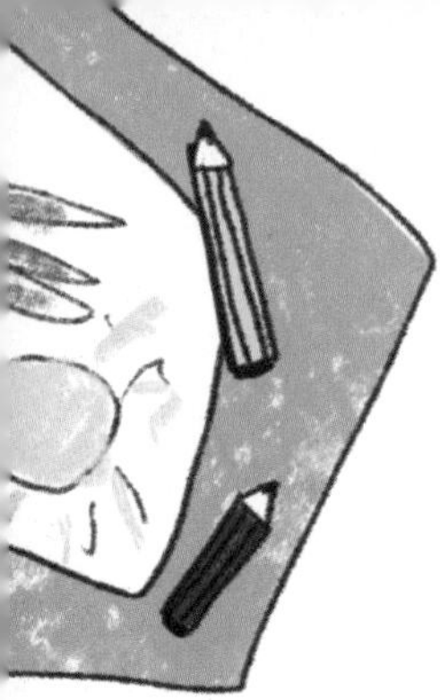

One of my favorite times at school, however, was when it was raining, which is unusual for me because I love dry, sunny weather. But when it was raining at school we didn't have to go to the loud, boisterous playground for recess and lunch; we were instead told to stay in the classroom for "wet day play," i.e., we remained at our desks and drew pictures.

This was the biggest relief to me. I didn't understand why we couldn't just stay at our desks and draw pictures all the time. Surely children running around the playground, screaming and falling over was a lot more dangerous than sitting down and drawing a nice picture of a cat?

So, yes, I could not concentrate in the classroom, yet I was desperate to do well with my studies. This led me to take every piece of classwork home to finish or improve. And it led to me staying up late every night to complete homework tasks, never quite knowing when they were actually finished (normally a long time before I'd stopped working on them).

One day when I was ten, my mom phoned the school to speak to my teacher. She was worried about the amount of homework I was being given and how tired I was from late nights working at my desk. The teacher told my mom that I was not being given a huge pile of homework at all. I was, in fact, making work for myself by "gilding the lily" (whatever that means). She said that I didn't need to be working as hard as I was, and that I should pay less attention to the presentation of my work and focus on the content.

This, quite frankly, upset me. I loved to draw and hand-design titles and decorative elements. I didn't want to give this up and hand in boring, bland work.

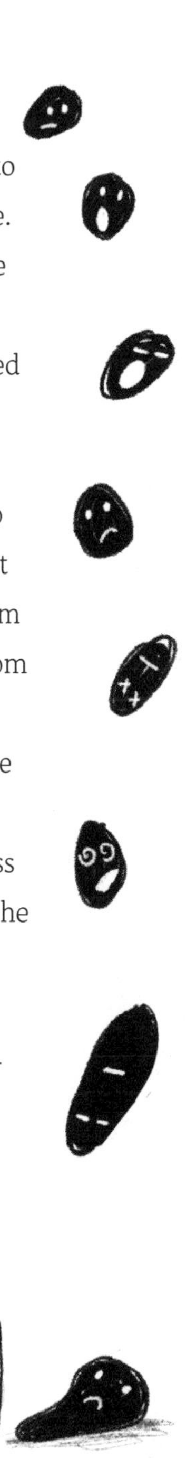

PERFECTIONISM

the need to be, or appear to be, perfect

And I don't think I ever did give this up, even after teachers said I should. I always felt that words and pictures together were the best things to look at. I needed both my writing and my art to tell one story. Just as I do today.

It wasn't enough to hand in a five-page report on my trip to the Mary Rose Museum; I had to sketch that boat as accurately as possible too, studying the library book I had taken out especially for this purpose.

Sometimes I would focus so intently on the elaborate detail of certain school tasks that I would get a mental block about others. Usually the duller, less creative tasks, which would take me much longer to produce . . .

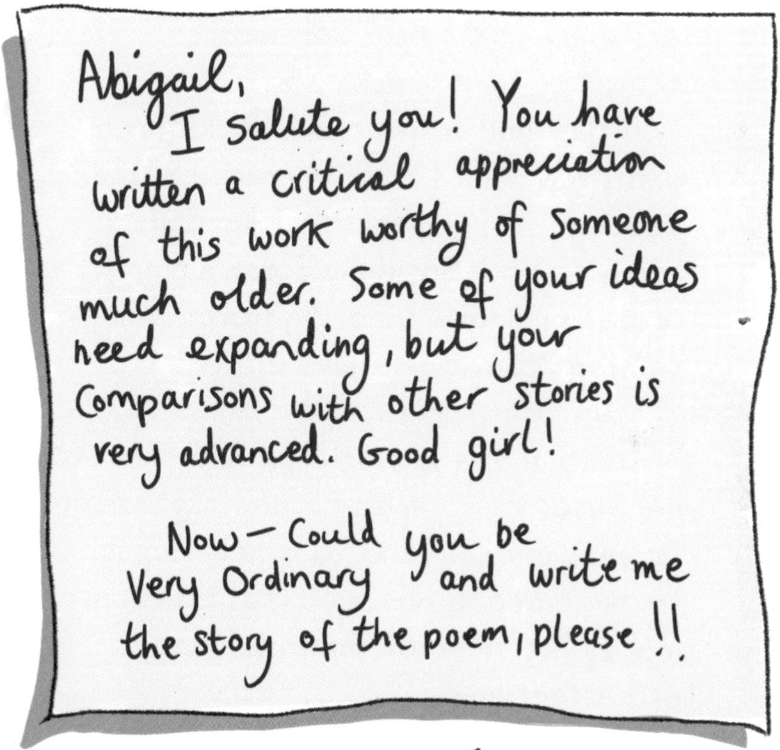

Abigail,
I salute you! You have written a critical appreciation of this work worthy of someone much older. Some of your ideas need expanding, but your comparisons with other stories is very advanced. Good girl!

Now – Could you be Very Ordinary and write me the story of the poem, please!!

Yes, my teacher actually asked me to be "very ordinary" because I hadn't completed a simple task she had set, yet I had completed something a lot more involved!

To my fourth-grade teacher,

Just writing to let you know that I now have a book out, called *A Different Kind of Normal.*

You can find it in actual bookstores and it combines both my writing and doodles, so I'm very glad I didn't listen to you. Basically I don't plan to be "ordinary" and I'm never going to stop "gilding the lily" either.

Also, PS that's a stupid phrase because it's so specific and lilies are flowers people send to other people when someone has died, so it just makes me think of funerals instead of perfectionism.

Best regards,

Abigail Balfe

XXX

Since I did my best work at home in the silence of my room, you might be able to guess how I did on class tests. Well, actually, when I was ten I was always top of the class for math tests. But that was because I was **SO** terrible at doing addition on the spot that I copied my friend who sat next to me. I felt super guilty about this, but I knew the alternative was getting zero out of twenty, and I couldn't risk the humiliation.

Back then, children were shamed for getting low results on tests. In my French class when I was fifteen, we had to read out our test results, and anyone with grades below a certain number had to stay behind for detention. My friend **George**[18] would beg me each week not to tell the teacher the truth about her low marks. Apparently my response was to look at her disapprovingly, shake my head, and say:

I'd forgotten about my own math-test escapades by then, conveniently . . .

18. George asked me to name her here. Because we are still friends today, twenty years later. Sorry I couldn't fit you into the friendship-list section, George. Blame my editor. (I always do, apparently.) I hope this footnote will make up for it.

BUT I always got top grades on spelling tests during school and didn't need to copy anyone for those. In fact, I was top of the class every week for months when I was nine, and I ended up winning several fountain pens. Ten years later, aged nineteen, I was even on a TV game show, **The Great British Spelling Test.** I was eliminated pretty soon into the game, though, because—surprise, surprise—I didn't perform well under pressure.

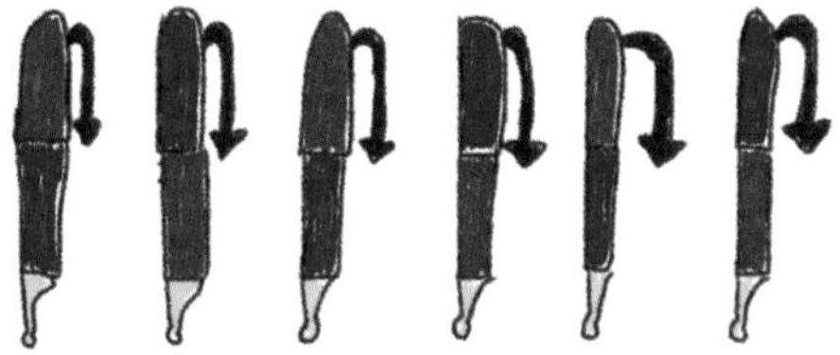

SEE: there is no set rule for how an autistic person may react to, or perform in, their environment. I didn't think anything could stop me from being good at spelling tests, but it turned out that being **on TV** doing spelling tests was my limit.

Nothing could make me like words any less, though. Words have always been important to me. I like the shapes they make. The spaces between them. And the stories they tell. I had an above-average reading level throughout school and loved to read about older children with normal-yet-exciting lives. Lives that I could aspire to lead one day.

I enjoyed writing fictional stories too and I still do. I actually imagined that **A Different Kind of Normal** would be a fictional book based on my life and the person I thought I wanted to be (but realized as I grew up that I could be whoever I want—and so can you!). Here's an **EXCLUSIVE** look at a very small section of the first draft.

A Different Kind of Normal: The Fiction Book (That Doesn't Exist)

I like reading. For me, it is like escaping my life for a few hours and becoming someone else. I read books about girls who go to school and get boyfriends and go shopping and wear makeup and have sleepovers. I imagine that I am one of those girls. One of those teenagers who glides through life understanding the rules, sharing identical worries about family and school and the color of their jeans and whether they match their socks.

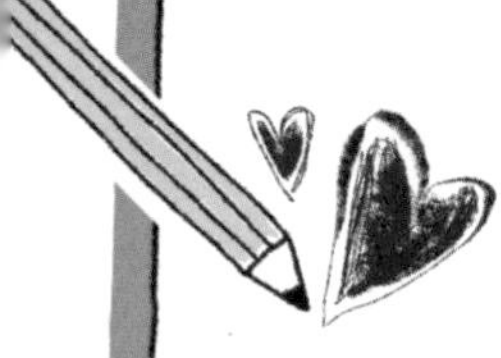

If I were a normal teenager, I would be called Bella. I would have long blond hair and a group of girl friends to have lunch with. We would do each other's hair in class and get in trouble for using our phones, and we'd run to the school fence at 3 p.m., hitching our skirts up and giggling when boys we liked walked past. I would be good at PE and play center on the netball team.

I'd get good grades, but not so good that I'd be considered a nerd. My parents would be happily married and I'd have a younger sister who looked up to me and copied how I dressed. I'd go to parties without telling my parents, kiss boys, and hide my phone in case a message from someone I liked popped up.

For a few hours I can believe I am that girl. But then Mom knocks on my door and tells me she can see the light of the flashlight that I'm using to read. I go to bed and back to worrying about another day at school feeling different.

Another day not understanding how
to be one of those girls.

MYTH: You can't really be autistic if you're academically skilled. If you are, you must be really **high-functioning**.

FACT: Autistic people can often have above-average intelligence. Many tend to excel at creative subjects such as art, drama, and music. The use of the labels **"high-functioning"** and **"low-functioning"** is damaging to autistics who manage to "pass" as neurotypical by hiding their struggles on a daily basis. The "low-functioning" label is also insulting to people with higher support needs. Instead, to show the range of autistic experiences, many prefer support labels, such as:

"I have zero/low/medium/high support needs."

These can also be tailored to specific circumstances, for example:

"I have zero support needs in academic work, but medium support needs when shopping in a supermarket."

It's very important to note here that the education system is often limited to just one way of teaching, which isn't terribly neurodivergent-friendly. We are all unique in the ways we learn and create.

As well as enjoying communicating with the written word, I love music and art with a passion. I taught myself how to play school songs on the keyboard and glockenspiel when I was seven, which led my parents to purchase a cheap piano and invest in piano lessons for me and my brother. This was a huge thing for us. We did not have a lot of money, but they wanted to support my talent.

Similarly my dad's mother was extremely poor when he was growing up, yet she scrubbed floors to save up and buy him a clarinet, which I ended up learning on too. Music has always been important to my family, and several of my family members have achieved great things in the music industry.

My parents' investment in my musical education really did pay off. During my final week at middle school we had an award-giving assembly, where I was presented with the Music Prize—a huge trophy and book voucher given each year to the pupil who had contributed the most to the school musically. People clapped and cheered and I performed a piano piece to the whole school, knowing that what I was doing was valued and approved of. It was probably the proudest moment of my life up until that point.

Communicating with music was, in a way, better and more powerful than communicating with words or pictures. I could feel it in every cell of my body. Taking over me, healing me, while entertaining those around me. I remember my mom saying to me that year: "You're going to find it very difficult to decide on a career, aren't you . . . ?"

(She was right.)

BIG SCHOOL

I was never scared by the idea of moving somewhere new. Somewhere no one would know me. Somewhere I could reinvent myself—**start fresh**.

My friends always thought this was weird, while I thought they were weird for feeling the opposite. When I left middle school I couldn't understand why the girls were all crying and hugging as they signed each other's T-shirts and yearbooks. Most of us would be going to the same high school anyway. Were they really going to miss this school? Or the lessons? Or the teachers?

The move to Big School was great. I felt pretty grown-up wearing my blazer and walking through the majestic old building, across the stone floor, and up the old-fashioned sweeping staircase. It felt important and atmospheric, like being in an old film or book.

Even though I'd get lost all the time looking for my locker, classes, and friends, I enjoyed the feeling of being at Big School. And I was doing well in all my subjects.

Well, apart from PE.

My time in PE at school consisted of me being told to

try harder

push myself

and

WAKE UP

as balls flew past my head and **sometimes**[19] into my face. I had little to no coordination and poor stamina, and was always picked last for team sports. I dreaded this class. Yet today exercise is so important to me. The silly thing is I had no idea at the time that there was a real **point** to physical education. I thought it was the most **POINTLESS** class in the world. When actually exercise can be **HUGELY** beneficial to our mental and physical health. Because there are so many ways in which we can exercise, it's sometimes a case of finding the right kind of exercise for **us**.

19. Often.

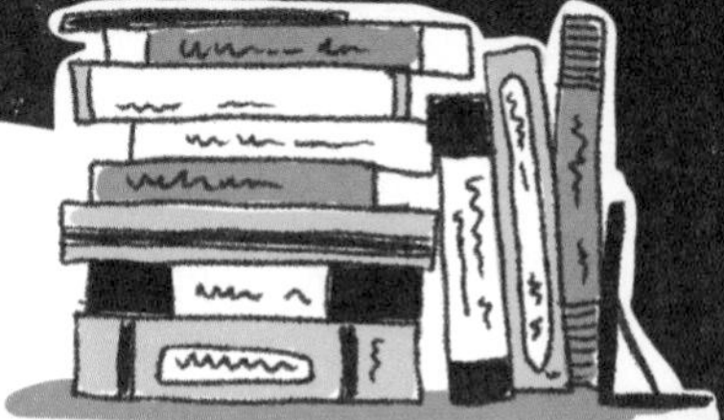

SCHOOL SUBJECTS:

a rundown

(I do NOT enjoy running! Why did I use that word?!)

HISTORY

I was very good at history because it is basically recounting facts. And I'm very used to relaying facts about things that have happened in my own life, such as my brother hiding my mom's dinner in a plant pot and my nana once suddenly deciding to meditate in the middle of a shopping center.

GEOGRAPHY

I was the teacher's pet. One year I won the Geography Prize even though I'd never been to another country, unless you count the Isle of Wight, but I don't think you do because apparently it's not another country—it might be just a part that fell off my country (England in the UK). Don't tell my geography teacher I said that. My favorite cloud is cirrus and today there is some light precipitation outside.

MUSIC

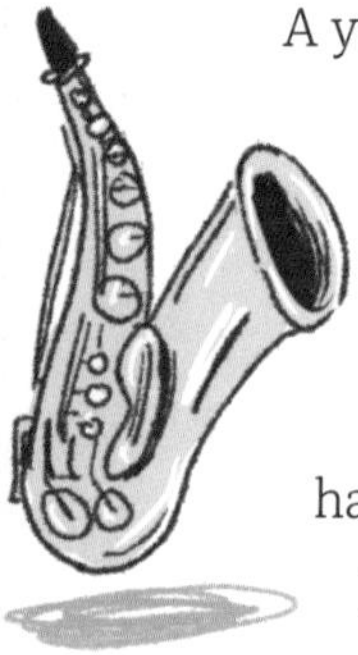

A year after winning the Music Prize in my final year at middle school, I also ended up winning the music subject prize in my first year at Big School. My music teacher loved me and I loved him. He would often let me sit in the school hall to practice on the grand piano instead of attending lessons because he knew there was not much I would learn in class. In reality, though, I learned so much from him and he was one of the most talented and inspiring teachers I've ever had. I was especially proud to be part of his orchestra, performing musicals he'd written to hundreds of people at the huge city theater two years running.

A few years later while at college I got my Grade 8 piano and took up music technology too, so I could learn to record my compositions. I recorded a song about killing a moth, but was disappointed to receive a C for it because I was confident that this song had the potential to be a number one hit on the radio or at least get me a five-minute comedy slot on some sort of important TV show.

ART

I think I'm pretty good at art in general, but I didn't always like being told what to draw. I'm skipping ahead a bit here, but when I started college-level art at age sixteen the teacher told us all to draw a boot he had placed on the desk. I got up and left the lesson because I had decided I would be a famous TV star soon anyway and I wouldn't need to draw a boot unless it was part of my TV character's story, which I highly doubted it would be, as most sitcom episodes are only half an hour long, while my art class was an hour long. Therefore I would've only really needed to know how to draw half a boot, if worst came to worst and my character was a boot-drawing art student.

Anyway, I didn't go back to that class except for one lunchtime with my friend (who now thinks she is autistic too) to tell the teacher to hold a frying pan while sitting in a shopping cart so we could take a photo. We got away with it as my friend was a photography student.

ENGLISH

I was good at this because I could write and read easily, and at a standard much higher than "normal" (whatever that means). I'm not trying to show off, by the way, I'm just telling you the facts. However, I realize sometimes when I write positive things about myself it can sound bigheaded, because people generally find it weird to openly talk about the things they are good at. I think we should all be able to champion our own successes just as easily as we seem to be able to talk negatively about ourselves, don't you?

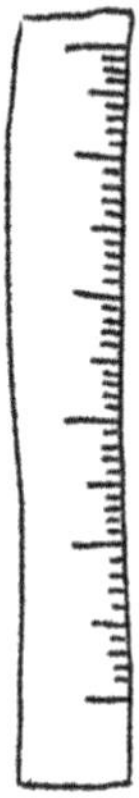

MATH

I considered math to be my worst subject even though I was in the top class. I was even given the option to take an extra course in statistics because (apparently) I was so good at math (but I didn't believe that one bit). Being the overworker that I was, I took the school up on the offer anyway and lived to regret it when it involved walking around supermarkets with a clipboard counting boxes of cereal and then failing the exam very badly because I couldn't (and still can't) add under pressure.

TECHNOLOGY

I studied textiles and during that time I made a pincushion with a robin on it. A few days later I told some people in my class that my mom was a Jehovah's Witness and that she had thrown away my pincushion because it was too Christmassy. (Jehovah's Witnesses don't celebrate Christmas.) I was testing my acting skills, as I was taking drama at the time, and they believed me. In the end I told them the truth (that my mom wasn't a Jehovah's Witness and that I still owned my pincushion) and I think **they** were impressed with my acting too. Though they could have also been embarrassed and annoyed. Hard to tell.

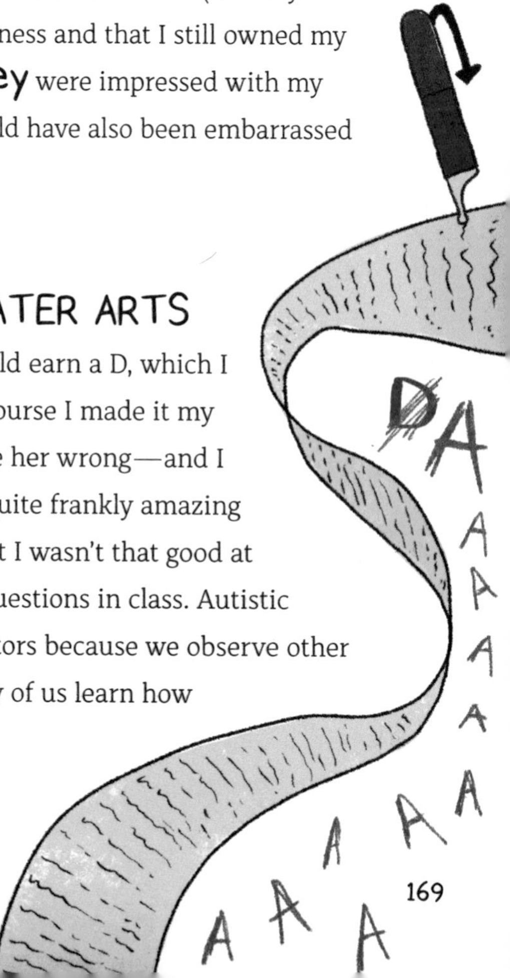

DRAMA AND THEATER ARTS

My teacher predicted I would earn a D, which I thought was **RUDE**, so of course I made it my mission to get an A to prove her wrong—and I managed it! I wrote some quite frankly amazing scripts and monologues, but I wasn't that good at group work or answering questions in class. Autistic people can be very good actors because we observe other people's behavior and many of us learn how to mask to fit in.

MASKING

Many autistic people mask their autistic traits in order to appear more acceptable to allistic people. Masking can involve **suppressing** repetitive behaviors (e.g., stimming), forcing eye contact, or using rehearsed phrases and tones of voice, and it can be done both consciously and subconsciously. People who are raised as girls are more commonly known to be good at masking, which can often delay them being diagnosed as autistic—if they are ever diagnosed at all.

When I'm acting I have a script, which means I can get totally absorbed in being the character I'm portraying. It's one of the few things that takes me away from my busy mind, and I find I get to a place where time passes quickly and effortlessly.

Acting often feels similar to the social mask I put on when meeting people in real life. (See the definition for "masking" above.) I can make myself into a larger-than-life character to start with, but I will often lose the ability to keep up the character as social events continue. These days I try not to mask if I can help it. But it can be hard to work out when I'm masking and when I'm being myself.

FACT: Masking can be harmful to an autistic person's health because it involves suppressing part of who you are. We should not feel as though we have to mold ourselves into something more acceptable to the outside world.

Learning how to unmask is something I am working on currently.

SCIENCE

I was scared of lots of things in science: Bunsen burners, cutting up animals, dead-animal organs, experiments where something shocking might happen, and having to work with people on experiments.

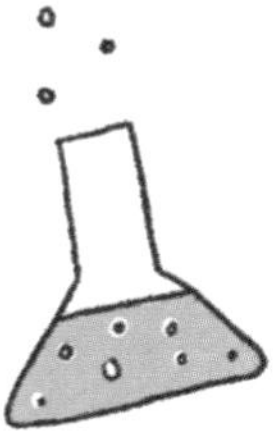

Even though I refused to take double science because I wanted to do art and drama, science is still pretty important, I think. It's because of science that we know things about the brain and autism. I took part in some research for science a few months ago and now I have some snazzy pictures of my brain.

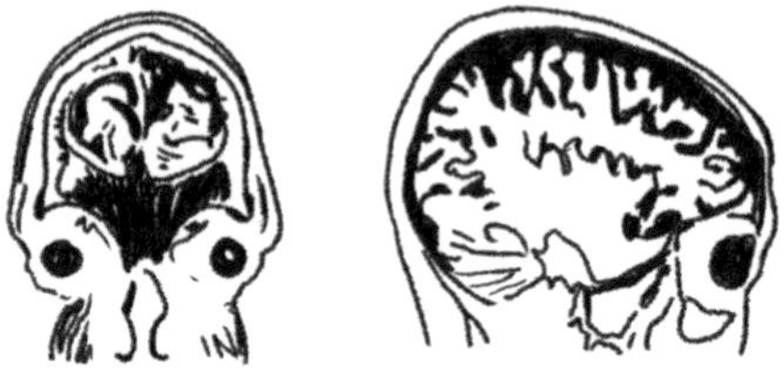

The brains of autistic people can sometimes look a bit different from the brains of allistic people. For instance, they can have decreased white-matter volume and larger ventricles. (Yes—very science-y terms!) There is evidence to suggest that autism might be able to be detected from an MRI scan one day. (An MRI scan creates photos of the brain, like mine up there!)

My ex-girlfriend said the gaps are where the thoughts should go. RUDE.

That's enough school subjects for now, as I was actually starting to tell you about changing schools, remember?

But before I continue . . .

MYTH: All autistic people have a special skill or hidden talent.

FACT: Some autistic people may be skilled or talented at certain things, but others might not. It doesn't matter if you're an eight-year-old professional pianist or a forty-year-old who cannot read without support and this book is being read to you. It takes all kinds of people, and indeed all kinds of autistic people, to make the world into what it is. And all our experiences and abilities are important and valid.

RIGHT, SO,

MOVING ON . . .

When I was twelve, my mom sat me down to tell me that she and my dad were getting divorced and I'd probably have to change schools again. I was strangely excited. Firstly, my mom was putting herself and me and my brother first. And, despite liking my school, I also enjoyed the idea of reinventing myself again. Maybe **this** time I could fool people into thinking I was cool and popular and confident. Maybe **this** time I could make people think I was **normal** . . .

Sadly it didn't work out that way. I changed schools during the spring when I was thirteen—and it was tough. Friendships had already formed without me, the school year was in full swing, and classrooms were noisier and more out of control than I had ever experienced. I could not cope with the disruptive behavior of my classmates, or the fact that the teachers knew nothing about me, and I was too overwhelmed to speak to them.

I was given free school lunches, which meant I had to sit on my own in the loud, busy—yet very small—cafeteria to choke down my chicken tenders every day, trying not to look anyone in the eye. (I became a vegetarian a few months later . . . perhaps the chicken tenders helped me make that decision. I am now a vegan, by the way, because I love animals even more than I did when I was a child!)

Once my mom was making my lunches again I would go to sit in the soundproof music room to eat them. Eating was forbidden there and I was always on edge in case a teacher saw me through the window. But it was better to be alone and on edge in a quiet room than it was to sit among a large group of boisterous children who I assumed didn't like me. I would take a bite of my sandwich, then hide it on my lap, pretending to be looking at my piano music.

I found it very difficult to make friends in my first year at this school, but there were a couple of girls I did get close to, who even came over to my house sometimes after school. They were, I guess, in the "misfits" category too. They both wore thick black eyeliner and listened to grunge music. And of course I ended up doing the same. So did my brother. He was better at putting on his eyeliner than I was.

A lot of the time the girls would end up hanging out with my brother in his room and I'd be left in my room, not knowing how to join in. I used my brother as entertainment, making him do silly things to amuse my friends.

But sometimes that would backfire, and they would want to hang out with him instead of me.

This painting is quite a sad, possibly slightly pathetic picture, SO instead I will paint you a happy, less pathetic picture of . . . a uterus and fallopian tubes!

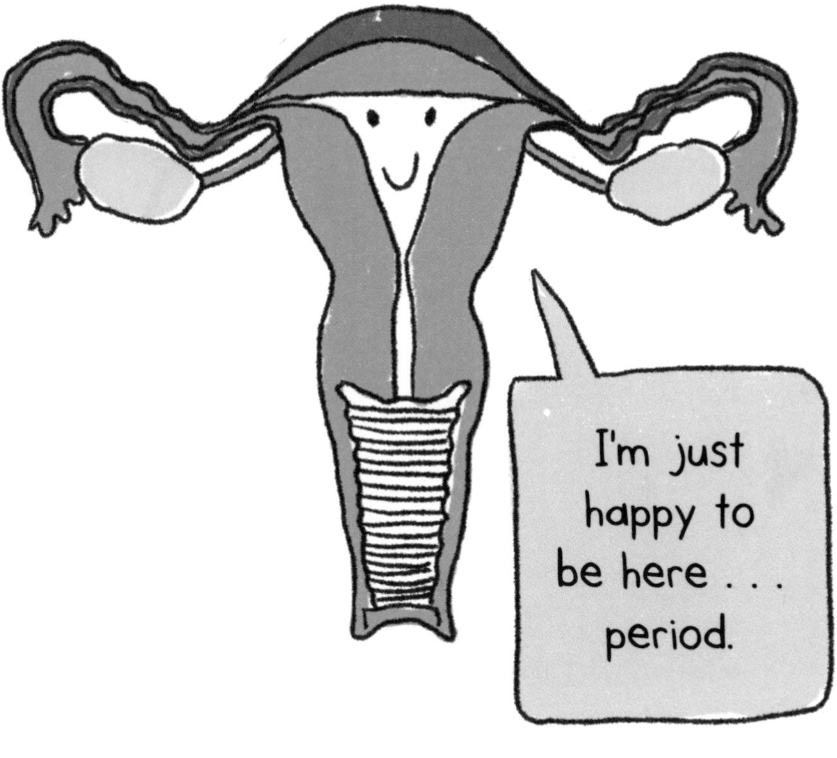

This has reminded me of another significant thing that happened around the same time as the unfortunate change of schools . . .

PUBERTY

When my mom first tried to teach me about puberty, I was not at all interested. It wasn't that I was embarrassed or felt awkward in any way; it was more that I found it incredibly boring. (Sorry, Mom.) Even though my mom made a big effort in her sex education lesson, using her big anatomy book and a (quite well-drawn) homemade sketch of genitalia, I did not see how any of it was relevant to me. I was a nine-year-old child and I just couldn't relate to anything she was talking about.

A few months later, I had to listen to the talk again from a teacher, so it was pretty good for me that my mom had already told me about it. Especially as it can take a few repetitions of something before I hear it, let alone understand it. Sometimes I watch TV shows twice because the first time I haven't understood and probably missed about 60 percent of the words spoken. (I'm not good at absorbing spoken information. It's an autism thing.)

I actually liked the talk about sex education by the time I heard it again from the teacher. The "boys" and "girls" were separated so the girls could learn about periods and the boys could learn about well, who knows? I wasn't there. But it felt special to me, like being in a secret sleepover club.

However, looking back, I realize that all genders should have learned the same things at the same time. It should be everyone's responsibility to understand the reproductive system and all its parts—that way we can learn about respecting each other and be more sensitive to each other's needs and feelings.

These days I think things are done a little differently, thankfully. But back then, similar to the way classes were divided by gender for sex education, autism was something people around me assumed was a male thing. Or, at best, they thought that if autism affected girls, it would affect every girl in exactly the same way.

As I write this, I'm aware I'm writing "boys" and "girls" in a very binary fashion again, because this is the way I was taught to think of gender at school. There was no education on the ins and outs of the gender spectrum.

As a young child I never considered that there could be more to gender than simply "boy" and "girl," and I also wasn't aware that romantic and sexual relationships could take place between gender identities other than one man and one woman.

I felt separate from binary "rules"—not knowing how wrong they were—which made me feel even more different. There has always been something that has felt a bit strange about the fact that I am a "girl." I looked at other girls at school and did not feel like I was "that" sort of girl. But I did not feel like one of the boys either.

I don't feel like a gender;
I FEEL LIKE MYSELF.

Yet I don't consider myself to be non-binary (any gender identity which does not fit the male and female binary) either. When someone refers to me as a "girl" or a "woman" it makes me laugh, yet I am happy to tick the "female" box on application forms. Sometimes I wear makeup, dresses, and nice shoes; other times I wear shirts, tracksuits, and sneakers. Sometimes I feel like an eighty-year-old woman, while other times I feel like a twelve-year-old child. But I am OK with this.

Although I find the idea of being a specific gender slightly odd, I don't feel the need to identify with an alternative label. But many autistic people do.

GENDER DYSPHORIA

The distress caused by the feeling that one's gender identity is not reflected in one's physical body.

TRANSGENDER

A person whose gender identity is different from the gender they were assigned at birth, based on their assigned sex at birth. Here "sex" refers to the biological differences between males and females, such as the genitalia, which is also a spectrum in itself (see "intersex," opposite). Whereas "gender identity" refers to how a person feels and their own concept of themselves. "Trans" is often used as shorthand for transgender.

A 2019 study carried out by Anglia Ruskin University (where I studied for my MA in Children's Book Illustration) discovered that transgender and non-binary people are "significantly more likely" to be autistic or display autistic traits than the wider population.

Perhaps this is because inquisitive autistic brains are more likely to hunt down answers to complex questions about gender identity? Or could it be that we are less willing to accept the rigid rules that the "normal" world tries to impose on us?

Either way, it's clear that the autistic population is made up of a variety of humans across the vast and varied gender spectrum, so I think it's important not to make the mistake of gendering autism (i.e., saying certain autistic traits belong to one gender). We can, however, notice the way traits can differ across the gender spectrum, just as they can across our differing personalities and due to our different backgrounds and environments.

I don't know if there were any transgender or intersex people in my class or whether anyone there would later identify as a different gender to the one they'd been assigned, but those perspectives and possibilities were entirely left out of my education. If anyone in my class was trans or intersex, they wouldn't have received the relevant information on how their body might develop, which is just not good enough really, is it?

INTERSEX

A term used for a variety of conditions where a person is born with a reproductive or sexual anatomy that doesn't fit the typical definitions of male or female. A person born with anatomy that does fit the typical definitions of male and female can be known as perisex.

See, because gender is such a big and important subject, these pages are quickly filling with fact boxes and thoughts that I didn't even realize I would be writing about when I first had the idea to make this book! I have tried to talk about sex and gender where it is relevant, but because I can't write everything about everything in this book, there are some brilliant resources out there where you can find helpful information and support. I've included some in the Really Useful Further Learning section at the back of this book.

OH YES . . . PUBERTY!

I was a couple of months away from turning thirteen when I first got my period. And I was very pleased about it when the day finally came. It meant I was growing up! And maybe it **also** meant that one day soon I would start to feel "normal" . . . like a real girl? Maybe even a woman?!

I didn't know how to tell my mom at first, because for some reason I felt like periods were something to be embarrassed about. How ridiculous is that?! They're something that happens to around half of the world's population for around seven days out of every month. They are a necessary part of reproduction. How could such a natural part of human existence ever be thought of as embarrassing?!

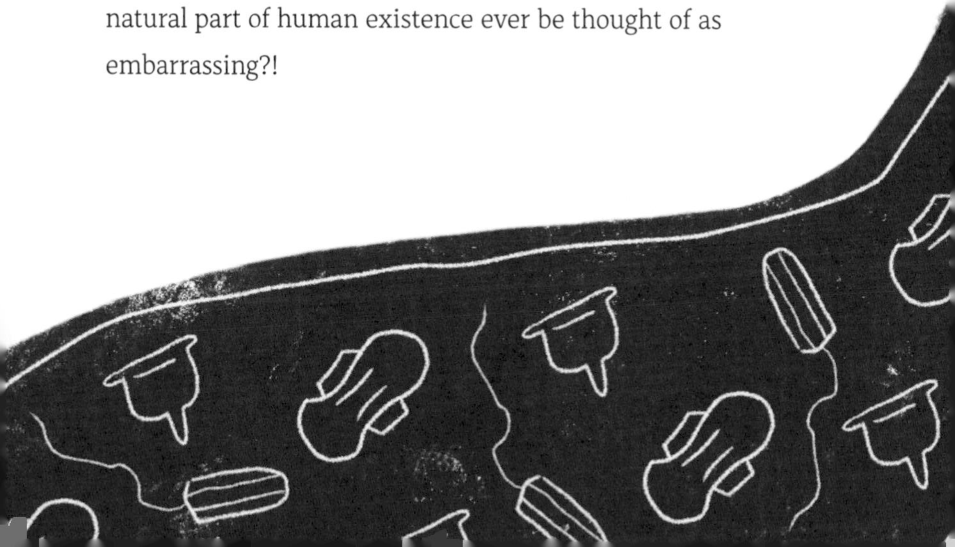

These days, thankfully, people talk about periods a lot more and sex education is slightly better than it used to be. However, I still see cisgender men looking grossed out at the mention of monthly bleeding and I know confident women who hide tampons up their sleeves before visiting the bathroom at work.

Let's TALK about periods
and make them feel NORMAL!

But let's also acknowledge they can be a bit poopy (quite literally sometimes—you'll probably need to use the toilet a lot more during your time of the month, but you'll get used to it).

Wearing a pad may not feel comfortable, especially if you are sensitive to sensory stimuli like I am. And the idea of putting something like a tampon or a menstrual cup inside yourself may feel scary, but these are things that are likely to become easier as you grow to understand your body and what works best for you. But if your period—or the idea of getting your period—distresses you, please talk to your primary care doctor about how you're feeling.

And if you're someone who doesn't get periods, there is no need to turn the page or look away.

Because everybody should learn about everybody.

Periods are nothing to be feared or dreaded. In fact, I quite enjoy having periods now that I know what to expect each month. It helps me feel grounded and part of the life cycle of this planet and the universe. Periods are a routine that I can organize my other life things around.

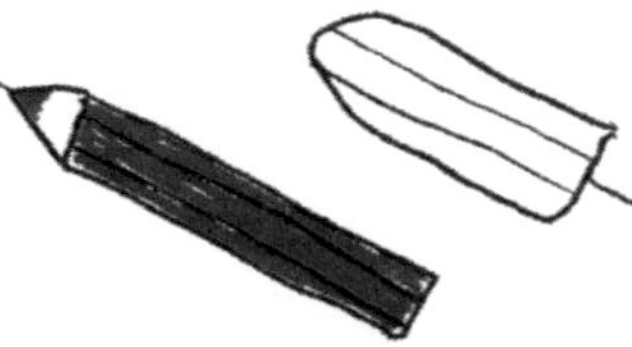

Yes, you may well have a day or two or three of mild to intense to very **intense**[20] pain, but this is **usually**[21] just a sign that your body is working and doing what it was designed to do.

When I started my period I didn't know how to tell my mom, so I created a game that allowed me to write it down instead of speaking. I told her I was going to try not to speak for several hours, a game I would sometimes play to see how long I could stay silent. This particular time, I wrote her the occasional message on a piece of paper. When I felt that it had been long enough, I went upstairs and prepared my next message.

20. Sorry, the word count of this book isn't large enough to delve into the delightful areas of endometriosis, adenomyosis, and polycystic ovary syndrome (PCOS), but you can always ask a trusted adult or a doctor for more information.

21. Or it could be an indicator of one of the above.

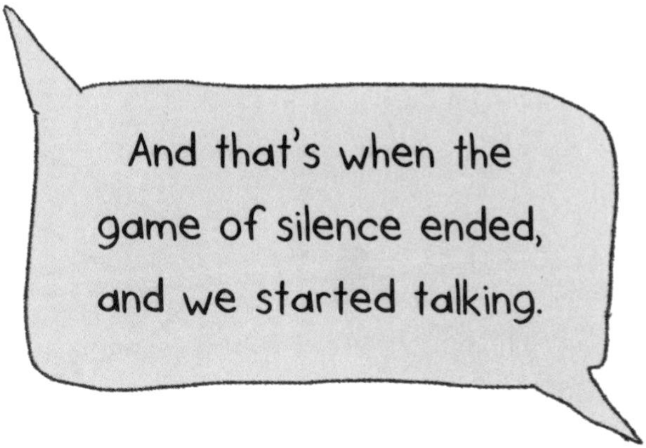

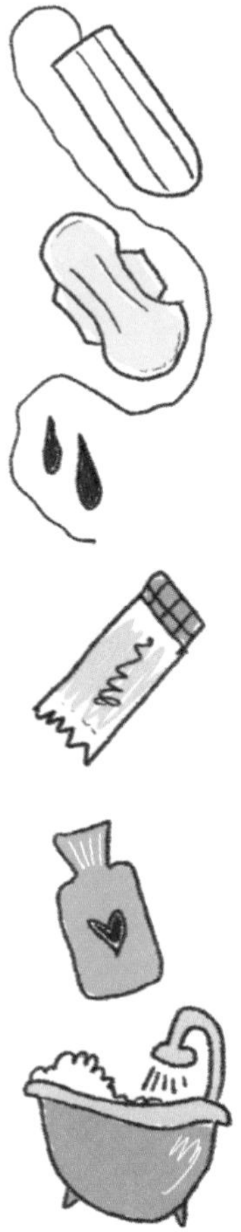

Although there was no need for me to feel embarrassed about discussing my period, as we know, sometimes it is easier for autistic people to communicate in other ways than talking out loud in sentences. Some of us may prefer the written word, some may be good at sign language, others may communicate through touch or movement or pictures.

Even though this world seems to have rigid rules when it comes to communication, remember: your brilliant self is more than capable of breaking those rules, and of creating rules that work for **YOU**. Your life is important. Your comfort and happiness are important.

And similarly, if you don't want to remove that new hair you find sprouting on various areas of your body, then don't! That person in the shaving ad was paid money to look that smooth on TV, don't you know.

And if you find that you're not feeling attracted to the gender that your best friend or parents think you should be attracted to, you don't have to question your feelings or force yourself to be attracted to them! Just like the gender spectrum, there is one of those for sexuality too. (Coming up in this book very soon . . .)

Puberty can be weird and messy and complicated, but the most important thing to remember during this time in your life is to follow your gut and trust your feelings. We[22] autistics can be pretty impressionable. When I was

22. I know there will be plenty of not-autistic people reading this, but also I'm talking to the autistic and potentially autistic people. Basically I want to make everyone feel included. I do hope it's working?

going through puberty, I thought everyone around me had a better idea of what was right for me and my body and my mind than I did. I didn't trust my own judgment or my emotions and became a mirror of the people around me, yet I also felt like a complete outcast.

What I'm saying here is:

This time in your life won't last forever.

Looking back, as difficult as the physical and emotional parts of puberty can often be, it was my relationships with the people around me that I struggled with the most. I didn't relate to the other children at my school and it wasn't just because I was autistic. It became clear to me that I wasn't experiencing puberty in quite the same way as the people around me seemed to be . . . There was something else that was making me feel separate and alone.

I remember the first moment I thought,

Oh dear . . . maybe I'm gay.

I was fourteen. I don't remember what sparked the thought specifically, but after years of never "liking" a boy, this thought suddenly popped into my head.

My heart sank. I caught sight of my face in the mirror: pale skin, frizzy hair, wonky teeth. And I thought,

Is this what a lesbian looks like?

I thought of my future and how I'd never be able to have a "normal" family. And worse—what if people **FOUND OUT** I was gay? Because back then, a lot of people weren't supportive of the LGBTQIA+ community.

Then I stopped and this is what I thought:

OK, calm down, and let's think about this rationally . . .

You don't know anyone gay.

There aren't any gays on TV.

Everyone on the radio sings about straight relationships.

There's nothing about gayness in magazines or the local newspaper.

You don't even have a gay uncle.

Your parents are definitely straight.

Right.

So how could you be one if you don't know any?

It doesn't make sense.

There can't be many gay people in the world if I've not met any by the age of fourteen, so it's such a small chance that I could be one.

Why would I end up being one of those unfortunate people when I've always been such a good, well-behaved child?

No, I will definitely feel normal eventually.

I just need to try harder.

I just need to do what the other girls are doing.

I just need to fit in.

I just need to make more effort.

(Can you see a pattern forming?)

That night I mentally went through all the boys I could think of in my grade. I intended to pick one to like.

Yes, I thought it really could be that simple.

I needed to force myself to enjoy looking at and listening to a boy. A gross,
snotty,
stinky,
pubescent boy . . .

Ugh, why did boys have to be so ANNOYING?!

It would have been easier to pick a girl.

Kind of.

I mean, not SUPER simple, but at least girls were easier on the eye. And at least girls were more . . . well, fully formed. More human. And they smelled better. A LOT better. And they had nice hair. And nice eyes. And much nicer legs. And sometimes they could be fun to hang out with too.

Wow.

This was not going to be easy . . .

I made my choice. Thomas T., it was.[23] He was the only boy who had been in the same elementary school as me years before. He'd been there when I had more friends. He'd seen me away from this terrible school. And he lived near my nana. And most importantly: he didn't bully me.

So now I just had to help people find out I had a crush on him.

The next day at school I was in luck. In class after lunch it wasn't long before talk turned to boys.

"Who do you like, Abi?" the girls at my desk giggled. This time I didn't go red or stutter. I had a plan. I had my answer.

23. I just realized I changed this boy's name to the name of a fictional cartoon train. Autism stereotypes are following me everywhere!

And so they quizzed me, and eventually they said his name.

I smiled in what I hoped was a coy and convincing way.

Turns out I'd accidentally picked the same boy my friend liked. Typical. However, there was nothing I could do about it now. There would be no fighting over him. She was welcome to him. Like a good friend, I would stand back and do nothing. We agreed we both had good taste in boys. And that was that. Ideal.

School continued and I felt like I was making progress.

I had a second boy-crush plan, and I was putting it into action. I had started to realize it wasn't enough to just like one boy. Girls would often crush on pop stars and actors, calling them "hot" and "cute," so I figured I'd better get my story straight (lol) on this too.

Now, despite my love of performing music, I did not have a particularly varied music taste . . . Since I was twelve, the only thing I would listen to was the Spice Girls or, when the Spice Girls split up (devastated, btw), their solo stuff.

There was one male pop act, however, whose CD I did buy and listen to pretty regularly around the age of fifteen. British pop star Craig David.

You probably haven't heard of him, but take it from me—he was a very attractive guy. Nice, smooth skin, good songs, the ability to count the days of the week in the correct order. Yes, what more could a fifteen-year-old girl ask for?

I went about this one a bit differently.

I'd seen how the other girls did it . . .

This time I would be able to put my observations and research to good use.

So I drew Craig David's CD cover in my art sketchbook.

Craig David . . .

I stuck his CD cover up on my bedroom wall. And I mentioned his name quite a lot.

. . . CRAIG DAVID!

And, yes, I'm pretty sure everyone believed that I was straight—for a few weeks at least.

Even I started to believe it after . . . maybe . . . **seven days**? (Well, it was a great song.)

All of the above might make me sound like, well . . . a bit of a liar, right? How deceptive to make up these untrue stories about myself to try to appear "normal"?!

But, as I mentioned earlier, autistic people are usually extremely honest.

I wasn't lying. I was trying hard to be what I thought I should be. What the world had told me was normal. I was trying to **"fix"** the parts of my brain that I felt had somehow gone wrong.

I spent the next few years pushing my feelings down, trying to be like the girls I was hanging around with, the girls I saw on TV and in magazines, and it wasn't until I was twenty-one that I met two bisexual girls at college and realized I did not need to force myself to be straight any longer. They were proud to be who they were and talked openly about their sexuality. And it wasn't long before I did too.

I joined the LGBT society and in my second year I even held the role of LGBT Officer. I led trips to gay bars and clubs and was the first port of call for LGBTQIA+ students asking for help at the Student Union office.

I've had boyfriends, I've had girlfriends, and I've met some of the most amazing, unique, talented, kind, and cool LGBTQIA+ people out there—many of whom are also neurodivergent.

LGBTQIA+

A common abbreviation for the lesbian, gay, bisexual, transgender, queer, questioning, intersex, agender, asexual, and aromantic community. Also includes other gender and sexual identities such as pansexual, demisexual, and gender-queer. You can find these terms in the glossary at the back of the book.

MYTH: Autistic people don't want or need romantic or sexual relationships.

FACT: The autistic community includes aromantic and asexual individuals (those who have little or no interest in romantic and sexual relationships), just as the allistic community does. It also includes a wide range of other romantic and sexual orientations. Autistic people crave love just like everyone else and tend to have greater flexibility in the areas of sexual orientation and gender identity.

Many people on the autism spectrum do not sign up to binary definitions—like "gay" or "straight," "boy" or "girl"—yet we like structure in other more day-to-day, practical areas of our lives!

COLLEGE

Starting college at sixteen was the biggest, most positive change in my life. It allowed me to start embracing my own individuality. I finally started to meet people who were "weirdos"[24] like me, and people who were openly gay. The artists, musicians, geeks, and freaks who probably also struggled in high school—we found each other. And it wasn't an uphill struggle to form friendships. They kind of happened naturally.

24. I'm reclaiming this word now by the way. WEIRDOS UNITE.

Well, I say naturally. Most of them **actually** started after I handed out my bag of lucky poo. In fact, a few months ago a friend sent me a photo of the lucky poo I gave her, which is still stuck on one of the pages of her yearbook. And the person who perhaps treasured her lucky poo the most out of all of these, my friend Emma, has since been diagnosed as autistic herself.

Sometimes if we take the time to be ourselves, we create space for like-minded people and experiences to come our way. We don't have to struggle to make friends, to learn to be "normal," or to make ourselves part of societies we are not suited to.

One day the world will embrace

YOUR uniqueness,

YOUR power,

YOUR four-dimensional beauty.

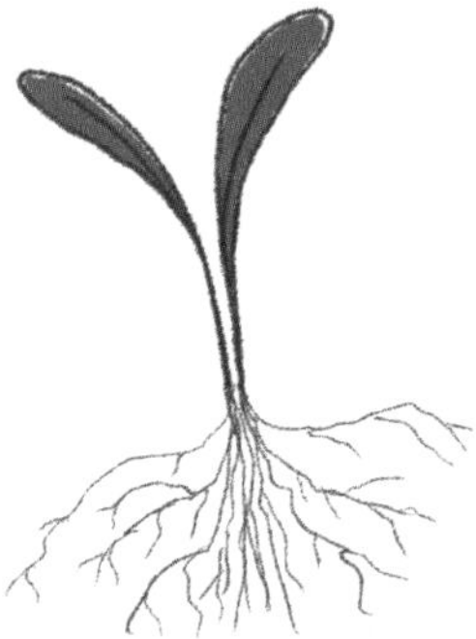

Because YOU are important

and YOU are worthy.

Just because you are YOU.

I'm not saying I don't still struggle with things. You just watch me try to deal with being in a busy London bar on a Saturday night. (Actually, don't—that'll make me more anxious.)

But what I am saying is that one day these things won't matter as much. As you grow up, your experience of the overwhelming world around you will grow and adapt too. And hopefully one day you'll suddenly realize that the things you once lost sleep over have become a little less painful, a little less important.

And even if you don't, that's OK too. There are no rules or deadlines when it comes to the way you move through your own life—only the rules you choose to create for yourself.

Choose the rules that help you grow, the rules that keep you safe, the rules that work for both you and those around you. Balance, kindness, and empathy are the most important things.

Make your own luck. Or use some of mine instead.

Trace and make your own poo here.

And so . . . we are almost at the end of my little book, which is now your little book. I hope my stories and facts have helped you understand some bits of life better, whether you are autistic or not.

I'm going to leave you now with some handy tips, further reading, and a glossary of important words.

Thank you once again, dear reader person, for joining me on this journey.

And can I tell you something before I go?

I'm excited for you.

Yes, really. I am.

Because your journey has only just begun.

I hope you are ready to
fully embrace your own

DIFFERENT
KIND OF
NORMAL.

MY TIPS FOR NAVIGATING THE NEUROTYPICAL WORLD IF YOU ARE NOT NEUROTYPICAL

FIND YOUR VOICE

Learn your communication likes and dislikes, and use those preferred ways of communicating in your daily life.

ASK FOR WHAT YOU NEED

In whatever way works best for **you**.

Your needs and desires are valid.

SET YOUR OWN BOUNDARIES

Work out what your limits and boundaries are, then stick to them.

FIND YOUR PEOPLE

Believe it or not, there are people like you out there; it's just a case of finding them.

GIVE YOURSELF A BREAK

You don't have to solve all the world's problems, or even your own, right now. Sometimes the best thing you can do for yourself and for the world around you is to rest and give yourself time to recharge.

MY TIPS FOR HELPING AN AUTISTIC PERSON FEEL SEEN

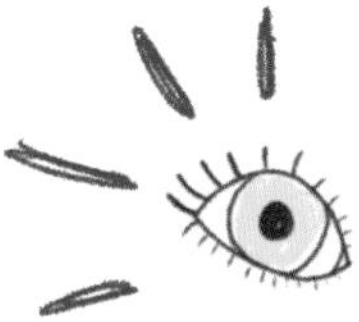

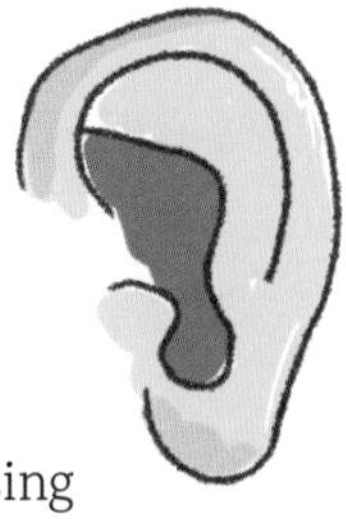

LISTEN

Create a safe space for them to express themselves, using whatever ways of communication work best for them.

GIVE

Be prepared to change your plans for them. Their need for structure or comfort may be greater than yours.

KNOW THEIR BOUNDARIES

Make sure they have control of their timetables and events. Their need to leave a situation is likely to be crucial to their health for the rest of the day or week.

HELP THEM EXPAND THEIR HORIZONS

Encourage and support them in their developing relationships and in their research around autism.

ALLOW THEM TO TAKE A BREAK

Space and silence are crucial for an autistic person. Their need for these doesn't reflect how they feel about you.

MY ABSOLUTE BEST THINGS ABOUT BEING AUTISTIC

kindness toward animals and humans

unique sense of humor

ability to think outside the box

excellent hearing

even more excellent ear for music

creative mind

art skills

childlike innocence

intuition and psychic abilities

youthful mind (and face apparently)

hyper-focus on work and creative projects

very cool and unique dress sense (yes, I write my own reviews)

A FINAL NOTE

I was diagnosed as autistic at age thirty-three, while studying for an MA in Children's Book Illustration. Being back in the classroom after many years sparked all sorts of feelings and memories, and it was one big catalyst[25] for me researching autism and eventually seeking a diagnosis.

Fortunately being in the MA program gave me a creative outlet for this journey and a way to tell my story. I started scribbling thoughts and facts and memories from my childhood in my sketchbook, making sense of my life on paper with lines and color and something solid to grab hold of.

25. An event causing a change. I like this word because it has a cat in it and I like cats, as you know by now.

But I didn't just want to do this for myself. During my quest to discover my own "truth," I realized that many, many people were in a similar position to me—searching for answers years down the line, having believed until then that there was something seriously wrong with them. Only as adults are they now discovering that perhaps their brains just work a bit differently from the brains of the people around them.

Many young people and adults are currently missing out on an autism diagnosis due to stereotyping and factors out of their control, such as gender, race, and how much money they have. It is a privilege to receive a diagnosis, and I feel extremely lucky.

I was in my thirties before I started to realize that there might be an underlying reason for my "weirdness." I've always known I was "different." I didn't fit in as a child and I still don't now, but autism just didn't cross my mind.

Because I knew nothing about autism.

Now, however, I do.

Yet, I still sometimes feel like a fraud. As if perhaps I've invented being autistic in my mind. That I've somehow discovered this handy label that I've decided to stick to myself as a convenient excuse for feeling like an outsider. That I've cleverly tricked the doctors and psychologists by using a list of unrelated items, sewn together in an attempt to make sense of a life that cannot be explained on a three-page form.

But (and here's the important part)—it's absolutely 100 percent NORMAL to feel like this. I know this now.

This imposter syndrome is the result of trying so very hard, for so many years, to HIDE all the autistic traits I went to the doctor about in the first place. It's the consequence of masking my autism in order to appear "normal" to the outside world. And in some ways I must have been an expert at this, since no one really noticed my struggles.

Or, maybe not . . . I remember once when I was a teenager, my brother, who I spent more time with than anyone else in my life, called over to my mom:

Although my mom initially dismissed the idea of autism because she knew nothing about it other than how it is misrepresented in the media, I **do** actually think autism is like having a creative gene.

We are always creating. Creating safe spaces around us to protect ourselves from our harsh environments. Creating new versions of ourselves in order to please the world. But, I believe, more importantly, we are actually creating the possibility of a better, more accepting, and more caring world, just by being our natural, inquisitive, loving, and honest selves.

I often wonder if all autistic people are actually extraordinarily spiritual beings, not meant for this physical world, our souls too big to be captured within the confines of a funny little body with legs and arms and limited capabilities. Our experiences of the world transcending anything that the "standard" human brain (whatever one of those is) could comprehend.

I wonder if all autistic people are really much closer to source energy, our true "selves," than we realize. That we are so strongly tapped into the collective consciousness and lacking the same level of separation that those around us seem to experience. And, as a result, we feel all the more separate.

The irony!

I imagine a world where we don't need to categorize ourselves by neurotype, gender, sexuality, race, or religion. A world where there are no expectations or rules and where everyone simply exists in peace and harmony. A world where we are all allowed to simply **"be"** without judgment. And where simply "being" is enough.

But, until that day exists, I am learning to embrace the parts of myself that happen to fall into categories and under labels, and do this without shame.

I am proud to be a thirty-five-year-old queer autistic woman.

I am proud to be an Aries. A vegan. An introvert.
A daughter. A sister. A friend.

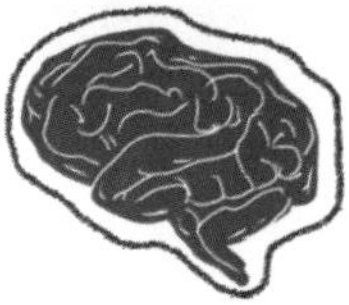

I am proud to have found communities where I feel accepted without judgment, where I can share my experiences openly and honestly with both like-minded individuals and those who are my strongest allies.

My autism diagnosis has helped me in ways I never thought possible. I now refuse to let my mental and emotional health take a back seat. I am important and I deserve to function in the way my mind, body, and spirit naturally call for me to function.

And so do YOU.

I've never been one for labels—I've found that these can often be restrictive and can fool us into thinking there are limits to our own magnificence. But autism is a label I can relate to. It explains my childhood, my teens, and my growing-into-an-adult years.

The word "autistic" is not placing limits on my abilities—it's giving me permission to continue to be as different and as creative and as genuine as I can be, knowing that is who I was meant to be in the first place.

I am proud of my past.
My present.
My future.
My achievements.
And my so-called mistakes.
I AM PROUD TO BE
ME.

I AM PROUD TO BE

A DIFFERENT KIND OF NORMAL.

REALLY USEFUL FURTHER LEARNING

There are lots of websites, blogs, and social media spaces that are great for learning more about autism. In fact, you may remember at the beginning of this book I told you how the internet provided me with the information, real-life stories, and connections that inspired me to seek my own diagnosis. But do check with a trusted adult before going online.

So let me tell you just a few of my favorites. I'll start with my own website because I hope there will be some things you might enjoy or relate to in my little corner of the internet too.

Active Minds
activeminds.org

The nation's premier nonprofit organization supporting mental health awareness and education for young adults

The Autism Society
autismsociety.org

A charity focused on empowering everyone in the autism community with the resources needed to live fully

Autistic Self Advocacy Network
autisticadvocacy.org

A nonprofit run by and for autistic people that seeks to advance and protect the rights of those with autism

Autistic Women & Nonbinary Network (AWN)
awnnetwork.org

A nonprofit organization providing community, support, and resources for autistic women, girls, transfeminine and transmasculine nonbinary and genderqueer people, trans people of all genders, Two Spirit people, and all others of marginalized genders

The Trevor Project
thetrevorproject.org

A nonprofit focused on mental health and suicide prevention for LGBTQ youth

"Autism in girls—I was wrong,"
Yo Samdy Sam

Sam, a cisgender autistic woman, reflects on the idea of "gendered autistic traits," suggesting a move away from the idea of female autism and male autism altogether—via Yo Samdy Sam on YouTube

"Autism Representation in the Media," *Toon Ruins*

A fascinating look at famous autistic people and TV characters, alongside some helpful autism knowledge and terms—via Toon Ruins on YouTube

"Autism Stereotypes and the Damage They Do to Autistic People," *Neurodivergent Rebel*

Lyric Holmans, a non-binary queer autistic person, discusses how stereotypes impact the neurodivergent community—via Neurodivergent Rebel on YouTube

"I'm Autistic, Black and Magical,"
Amina Mucciolo (aka Tasselfairy)

Amina answers questions about autism and what it's like to find out you're autistic as an adult—via her YouTube channel Tasselfairy

"Sometimes You're a Caterpillar,"
Chescaleigh

Learn about privilege and difference through this (very cute) short animated tale about a snail and a caterpillar—via Chescaleigh on YouTube

Can You See Me?, *Libby Scott and Rebecca Westcott*
People think that because Tally's autistic, she doesn't realize what they're thinking, but Tally sees and hears—and notices—all of it. A novel about autism, co-authored by an eleven-year-old autistic girl.

A Kind of Spark, *Elle McNicoll*
Eleven-year-old Addie campaigns for a memorial for the witch trials that took place in her Scottish hometown. Debut novel written by this neurodivergent author.

M Is for Autism, *The students of Limpsfield Grange School and Vicky Martin*
A fictional book written by the students of Limpsfield Grange, a school for autistic girls, drawing on their own real-life experiences

Planet Earth Is Blue, *Nicole Panteleakos*
A heartrending and hopeful story about a non-verbal girl and her passion for space exploration

The Someday Birds, *Sally J. Pla*
When his father must travel cross-country for medical treatment, an autistic boy faces a long road trip and abrupt change to his comfortable routine.

GLOSSARY

All words included in this glossary are ones that I haven't already defined in this book. I thought it would be useful to include these in this space, as they were all important in telling you my story.

Words change all the time, and while I've aimed to get the definitions for these terms as correct as possible during writing, there is a chance that some of the preferred terms and their meanings may have changed by the time this book finds its way into your life. For the most up-to-date conversations around autism, check out the National Autistic Society website.

ADHD (attention deficit hyperactivity disorder)—p. 15, p. 69
A neurodevelopmental condition involving a combination of persistent problems, such as difficulty sustaining attention, hyperactivity, and impulsive behavior. A form of neurodivergence.

Agender—p. 12, p. 202
A person who does not identify themselves as having a particular gender

Androgyne—p. 12
A non-binary gender identity that can be a blend of both binary genders—man or woman—or include neither. Androgynes can also identify as being between female and male, or as neither male nor female. Androgynes might also identify as transgender or gender-queer.

Aromantic (aro)—p. 202, p. 203
A term that describes someone who experiences little to no romantic attraction. It can also describe someone who doesn't feel romantic attraction in the way it's normally thought of by society. Aromantic is often abbreviated to aro.

Asexual (ace)—p. 202, p. 203
A term that describes someone who experiences little to no sexual attraction. It can also describe someone who doesn't feel sexual attraction in the way it's normally thought of by society.

Bisexual (bi)—p. 201, p. 202
A term that describes a person who experiences sexual attraction to two or more genders. A person who experiences romantic attraction to two or more genders is biromantic. Bi can be a short form for either term, or a general term that covers both.

Demisexual—p. 202
A sexual orientation where the person only experiences sexual attraction to someone that they have a close emotional connection with.

Diagnose—p. 13, p. 20, p. 68, p. 95, p. 170, p. 205, p. 216
Identify the nature of an illness or condition by examining symptoms or traits

Dyscalculia—p. 15
Difficulty in making arithmetical calculations, as a result of a brain disorder. A form of neurodivergence.

Dyslexia—p. 15
A learning difficulty involving problems with reading, writing, and spelling, but which does not affect general intelligence or creativity. A form of neurodivergence.

Dyspraxia—p. 15
A developmental disorder that affects movement and coordination. A form of neurodivergence.

Empath—p. 60

A person who is highly sensitive to the emotions of those around them, to the point of experiencing those emotions themselves

Gay (also homosexual, homoromantic, or queer)—p. 128, p. 193, p. 194, p. 195, p. 201, p. 202, p. 203, p. 204

A term for someone who only experiences attraction to the same gender as their own

Gender—p. 12, p. 13, p. 22, p. 25, p. 54, p. 55, p. 56, p. 179, p. 180, p. 181, p. 182, p. 183, p. 184, p. 190, p. 202, p. 203, p. 217, p. 220

Different from birth sex, gender refers to the characteristics of men and women that are socially constructed and involves how a person identifies. While many people identify as having a gender (for instance, man or woman, although these are only two of many genders), not everyone does—and you may find that your gender identity changes over time as you develop a stronger understanding of who you are.

Gender-fluid—p. 12, p. 55

A term for a person who does not identify themselves as having a fixed gender

Gender identity—p. 13, p. 181, p. 182, p. 203

Refers to a person's deeply felt, internal and individual experience of gender, which may or may not correspond to the person's physical characteristics or the sex they're given at birth

Gender-neutral—p. 12

A non-binary gender identity—people who identify as gender-neutral often have a neutral gender identity or expression, or prefer gender-neutral language and pronouns. This can be similar to the experience of being agender or neutrois.

Gender-queer—p. 12, p. 202

A term that is similar in meaning to non-binary. It can also be used to describe binary cisgender and transgender people within the LGBTQIA+ community who feel that they have an experience of gender that is different from what is considered "normal."

Imposter syndrome—p. 218

A name for feeling as if you are not good enough, even though others might think you are—whether it's in a job, school, or maybe in your social life

Lesbian—p. 193, p. 202

Refers to women who are attracted to women, and is now a broader term for someone whose gender identity relates to being a woman in some way, and who only experiences attraction to the same gender as their own

Mental health—p. 164, p. 221
The condition of a person's mind. It's important to look after our mental health, just as we would our physical health.

Neutrois—p. 12
A non-binary gender identity that is often associated with a "neutral" or "null" gender

Non-binary—p. 12, p. 181, p. 182
A term for a person whose gender doesn't fit into the gender binary of male and female. A non-binary person may identify as having no gender, one gender, or more than one gender.

Openly gay—p. 128, p. 204
Acknowledging that you are gay or lesbian. It is often associated with the term "coming out," the process of informing other people that you are not a heterosexual, heteroromantic, cisgender, perisex person. (These are, unfortunately, what general society dictates as "normal.") Some people do not come out to anyone, some only come out to people they're close to and feel safe with, some only come out to prospective partners, some only come out online, and some people are out to the general public (like LGBTQIA+ celebrities).

Pangender—p. 12
A term for a gender identity in which a person identifies as lots of separate identities that are fluid over time. The genders that a pangender person has only include genders within the person's own culture and life experience.

Period—p. 177, p. 179, p. 185, p. 186, p. 187, p. 188, p. 189
Most commonly refers to the point in the menstrual cycle where the lining of the uterus breaks away and exits the body through vaginal bleeding. This usually occurs for five to seven days in a row, at roughly monthly intervals. Some intersex people have periods that do not feature vaginal bleeding, so if you are intersex and experience abdominal cramps or mood changes you should talk to your doctor.

Primary Care Doctor—p. 187
A doctor based in the community who treats patients with minor or chronic illnesses and refers those with serious conditions to a hospital

Puberty—p. 178, p. 184, p. 185, p. 190, p. 191, p. 192
A biological process in which sex hormones (substances that affect how a body behaves) begin to change the way a young person's body develops as they become an adult. These changes vary across genders and can involve developing breasts, starting periods, growing body hair, and growth spurts.

Queer—p. 201, p. 202, p. 220

A term used by many people across the LGBTQIA+ community, and across the LGBTQIA+ spectrum, for those who want to go by that label. Historically used as an offensive term, it has been reclaimed by many as an empowering and liberating term, though it can still trigger upset in some people.

Questioning—p. 202

A term referring to those who question their gender identity, romantic orientation, sexual orientation, or sex. Questioning people are included under the Q of LGBTQIA+, along with people who identify as queer.

Reproductive system—p. 179

The internal and external organs involved in producing offspring, including the uterus, ovaries, fallopian tubes, vagina, penis, scrotum, and testes

Sensory anxiety—p. 90

Anxiety caused by the stress that comes from expecting certain sensory stimuli (such as loud sounds, bright lights, and/or strong smells)

Sensory stimuli—p. 93, p. 187

Any events or objects that are received by our senses. This includes things you hear, smell, taste, or touch.

Sex—p. 13, p. 182, p. 184

Based on biology, sex is a spectrum, and is affected and defined by chromosomes, hormones, genitals, and reproductive systems. A person's sex refers to where that individual falls on the spectrum, and may differ from the sex they were assigned at birth. It is not limited to male and female. (See the Intersex fact box on page 183.)

Sexual orientation—p. 203 (sometimes referred to as sexuality—p. 190, p. 201, p. 220)

A person's identity in relation to the gender or genders to which they are/are not sexually attracted

Spectrum—p. 12, p. 15, p. 22, p. 180, p. 182, p. 183, p. 190, p. 203

A term used to classify something in terms of its position on a scale between two extreme points, e.g., the gender spectrum, the sexuality spectrum, and of course, the autism spectrum

Straight (also heterosexual or heteroromantic)—p. 194, p. 200, p. 201, p. 203

A term for someone who only experiences attraction to a different gender from their own

Tourette's syndrome—p. 15

A neurological condition that causes a person to make involuntary sounds and movements called tics. A form of neurodivergence.

ACKNOWLEDGMENTS

Oh, is this the part where I make a thank-you speech like I'm at an awards ceremony? OK!

Right . . . I am now visualizing myself wearing a fancy dress with fancy sneakers (because I might fall over in heels), and I'm standing up on a huge stage proudly holding this book instead of a trophy. Or maybe I'm holding a trophy in the shape of my book? A book-shaped trophy made of GOLD! YES!

OK, I'm getting distracted.

I'd like to thank . . .

Firstly, thank you so, so much to everyone at Puffin, in particular commissioning editors Tom Rawlinson and Emily Lunn, for believing in my story enough not only to give me my first-ever (two-book!) publishing deal, but also to select *A Different Kind of Normal* as their lead nonfiction launch of 2021. It's an absolute honor and a privilege—and also very surreal! I would pinch myself, but I'm very sensitive to pain so instead I will continue writing these words.

Thank you again to my lovely, patient, kind editor, Tom. You've been so supportive throughout this whole process in so many ways and it's been a joy to work with you on this.

Thank you to my talented designer, Stephanie Jones. In particular for bringing the cover to life in new ways and for your patience and encouragement as I drip fed you artwork at 3 a.m. every night!

Stephanie Barrett, Ellen Grady, Beth O'Brien, Michelle Olvera, plus everyone else behind the scenes at Puffin who I might not have met—thank you!

Thank you to my US publishing team at Crown Books for Young Readers and my team in Canada, Tundra Book Group. And to both teams, thank you for understanding that a story like mine crosses geographic and political boundaries.

Thanks to Inclusive Minds (the CIC supporting and championing inclusion and diversity in children's books) for introducing us to Jo, Louise, and Pooja, through their network of Inclusion Ambassadors. And thank you to Jo, Louise, and Pooja—your knowledge, wisdom, and suggestions have been invaluable and I'm so grateful for your input.

A very big thank-you to my wonderful agent, Emily Talbot, at United Agents, for first reaching out to me when I was graduating from my MA, for securing my first book deal, and for managing all the other things that I would probably find quite difficult to do alone.

My MA Children's Book Illustration tutors and lecturers at Cambridge School of Art, especially Katherina Manolessou, Paula Metcalf, Marta Altes, Birgitta Sif, Viola Wang, Pam Smy, Becky Palmer, Hannah Webb, and Martin Salisbury. Thank you for all your wisdom and guidance. I learned so much from you and taking the course was one of the best decisions I've ever made.

Thank you to Mum for believing in me and for always being proud. Dad and Nan for being around me in spirit. And my brother Patrick for teaching me lots about life and myself without even trying.

Thank you to Rachel for all of the love, support, and the hundreds of meals on the red cushion.

And lastly, and very importantly, thank you to YOU, dear reader person. For picking up this book.

And for just being you.